50 Family Gathering Recipes for Home

By: Kelly Johnson

Table of Contents

- Grandma's Pot Roast
- Mom's Meatloaf
- Dad's Grilled Chicken
- Aunt Martha's Lasagna
- Cousin Sarah's Macaroni Salad
- Uncle Joe's BBQ Ribs
- Sister Emily's Chocolate Chip Cookies
- Brother Mike's Buffalo Wings
- Grandma's Apple Pie
- Mom's Chicken Parmesan
- Dad's Steak and Potatoes
- Aunt Martha's Tuna Casserole
- Cousin Sarah's Cornbread
- Uncle Joe's Pulled Pork Sandwiches
- Sister Emily's Brownies
- Brother Mike's Guacamole
- Grandma's Chicken Soup
- Mom's Spaghetti and Meatballs
- Dad's Chili
- Aunt Martha's Beef Stew
- Cousin Sarah's Caesar Salad
- Uncle Joe's Baked Beans
- Sister Emily's Banana Bread
- Brother Mike's Nachos
- Grandma's Pancakes
- Mom's Quiche
- Dad's Grilled Salmon
- Aunt Martha's Potatoes Au Gratin
- Cousin Sarah's Spinach Dip
- Uncle Joe's Corn on the Cob
- Sister Emily's Lemon Bars
- Brother Mike's Salsa
- Grandma's Stuffed Peppers
- Mom's Eggplant Parmesan
- Dad's Paella

- Aunt Martha's Corn Chowder
- Cousin Sarah's Fruit Salad
- Uncle Joe's Coleslaw
- Sister Emily's Rice Krispie Treats
- Brother Mike's Deviled Eggs
- Grandma's Baked Ziti
- Mom's Beef Wellington
- Dad's Shish Kabobs
- Aunt Martha's Shepherd's Pie
- Cousin Sarah's Garlic Bread
- Uncle Joe's Crab Cakes
- Sister Emily's Oatmeal Cookies
- Brother Mike's Cheese Platter
- Grandma's Cinnamon Rolls
- Mom's Lemon Chicken

Grandma's Pot Roast

Ingredients:

- 1 (3-4 pound) beef chuck roast
- Salt and pepper, to taste
- 2 tablespoons vegetable oil
- 1 onion, chopped
- 3-4 cloves garlic, minced
- 4 carrots, peeled and cut into large chunks
- 4 potatoes, peeled and cut into large chunks
- 2 cups beef broth (low sodium if possible)
- 1 cup red wine (optional)
- 2-3 sprigs fresh thyme (or 1 teaspoon dried thyme)
- 2-3 sprigs fresh rosemary (or 1 teaspoon dried rosemary)
- 2 bay leaves

Instructions:

1. Preheat your oven to 325°F (160°C).
2. Season the chuck roast generously with salt and pepper on both sides.
3. Heat the vegetable oil in a large Dutch oven or heavy-bottomed pot over medium-high heat. Sear the roast on all sides until browned, about 4-5 minutes per side. Remove the roast from the pot and set aside.
4. In the same pot, add the chopped onion and cook until softened, about 3-4 minutes. Add the minced garlic and cook for another 1-2 minutes until fragrant.
5. Deglaze the pot with the red wine (if using), scraping up any browned bits from the bottom of the pot.
6. Add the beef broth, fresh thyme, rosemary, and bay leaves to the pot. Bring to a simmer.
7. Return the seared roast to the pot. Arrange the carrots and potatoes around the roast.
8. Cover the pot with a lid and transfer to the preheated oven. Cook for about 3-4 hours, or until the roast is fork-tender and the vegetables are cooked through.
9. Once cooked, remove the pot from the oven. Transfer the roast to a cutting board and let it rest for about 10-15 minutes before slicing.
10. Serve the pot roast slices with the vegetables and a ladle of the flavorful cooking juices.

Enjoy Grandma's Pot Roast with your loved ones for a hearty and satisfying meal!

Mom's Meatloaf

Ingredients:

- 1 lb ground beef (preferably lean)
- 1/2 lb ground pork (or use all ground beef if preferred)
- 1 cup breadcrumbs (plain or seasoned)
- 1/2 cup milk
- 1 onion, finely chopped
- 2 cloves garlic, minced
- 1/2 cup grated Parmesan cheese
- 1/4 cup ketchup
- 2 tablespoons Worcestershire sauce
- 1 tablespoon Dijon mustard
- 1 teaspoon salt
- 1/2 teaspoon black pepper
- 2 eggs, lightly beaten

For the glaze:

- 1/2 cup ketchup
- 2 tablespoons brown sugar
- 1 tablespoon apple cider vinegar

Instructions:

1. Preheat your oven to 350°F (175°C).
2. In a small bowl, soak the breadcrumbs in milk and set aside.
3. In a large mixing bowl, combine the ground beef, ground pork, soaked breadcrumbs (squeeze out excess milk), chopped onion, minced garlic, grated Parmesan cheese, ketchup, Worcestershire sauce, Dijon mustard, salt, pepper, and beaten eggs. Mix well using your hands or a spoon until all ingredients are evenly combined.
4. Transfer the meat mixture to a lightly greased loaf pan, shaping it into a loaf shape.
5. In a separate bowl, mix together the ingredients for the glaze: ketchup, brown sugar, and apple cider vinegar. Spread half of the glaze evenly over the top of the meatloaf.
6. Bake the meatloaf in the preheated oven for about 45 minutes to 1 hour, or until the internal temperature reaches 160°F (71°C) using a meat thermometer.

7. About 10-15 minutes before the meatloaf is done, spread the remaining glaze over the top and continue baking until the glaze is caramelized and bubbly.
8. Remove the meatloaf from the oven and let it rest for about 10 minutes before slicing.
9. Slice and serve Mom's Meatloaf warm with mashed potatoes, green beans, or your favorite side dishes.

Enjoy this comforting and flavorful meatloaf recipe that reminds you of home and family gatherings!

Dad's Grilled Chicken

Ingredients:

- 4 boneless, skinless chicken breasts
- 1/4 cup olive oil
- 2 cloves garlic, minced
- 2 tablespoons fresh lemon juice
- 1 teaspoon dried oregano
- 1 teaspoon dried thyme
- 1 teaspoon paprika
- Salt and pepper, to taste

Instructions:

1. In a bowl or shallow dish, whisk together olive oil, minced garlic, lemon juice, dried oregano, dried thyme, paprika, salt, and pepper. This mixture will serve as the marinade for the chicken.
2. Place the chicken breasts in the marinade, ensuring they are well coated. Cover the dish with plastic wrap or transfer everything to a zip-top bag. Refrigerate and let marinate for at least 30 minutes to 2 hours. For more flavor, you can marinate overnight in the refrigerator.
3. Preheat your grill to medium-high heat.
4. Remove the chicken breasts from the marinade and discard any excess marinade.
5. Grill the chicken breasts for about 6-7 minutes per side, or until they are fully cooked through and have reached an internal temperature of 165°F (74°C). Cooking time may vary depending on the thickness of the chicken breasts.
6. Once cooked, remove the chicken from the grill and let it rest for a few minutes before serving.
7. Serve Dad's Grilled Chicken with your favorite sides such as grilled vegetables, salad, rice, or potatoes.

This recipe produces tender and flavorful grilled chicken that's sure to be a hit at your family gathering, just like Dad makes it!

Aunt Martha's Lasagna

Ingredients:

- 1 pound sweet Italian sausage, casings removed
- 1 pound ground beef
- 1 onion, finely chopped
- 4 cloves garlic, minced
- 1 (28-ounce) can crushed tomatoes
- 2 (6-ounce) cans tomato paste
- 1/2 cup water
- 2 tablespoons white sugar
- 1/4 cup chopped fresh basil (or 1 tablespoon dried basil)
- 1 teaspoon salt
- 1/2 teaspoon ground black pepper
- 1/4 cup chopped fresh parsley (optional)
- 12 lasagna noodles
- 16 ounces ricotta cheese
- 1 egg
- 3 cups shredded mozzarella cheese
- 3/4 cup grated Parmesan cheese

Instructions:

1. In a large skillet or saucepan, cook the Italian sausage, ground beef, onion, and garlic over medium heat until the meat is browned and the onion is tender. Drain excess fat.
2. Stir in crushed tomatoes, tomato paste, water, sugar, basil, salt, pepper, and parsley (if using). Simmer, uncovered, for about 45 minutes, stirring occasionally.
3. Preheat your oven to 375°F (190°C). Bring a large pot of lightly salted water to a boil. Cook the lasagna noodles according to package directions until al dente. Drain and set aside.
4. In a mixing bowl, combine ricotta cheese with the beaten egg.
5. To assemble the lasagna, spread a thin layer of meat sauce in the bottom of a 9x13 inch baking dish. Arrange a layer of cooked lasagna noodles lengthwise over the sauce. Spread with half of the ricotta cheese mixture. Top with a third of mozzarella cheese and a third of Parmesan cheese. Repeat layers, ending with remaining meat sauce, mozzarella, and Parmesan cheese.
6. Cover with aluminum foil (to prevent sticking, either spray foil with cooking spray, or make sure the foil does not touch the cheese).

7. Bake in preheated oven for 25 minutes. Remove the foil, and bake an additional 25 minutes. Let stand 10 to 15 minutes before serving.
8. Enjoy Aunt Martha's Lasagna with a side of garlic bread and a green salad for a delicious family meal!

This lasagna recipe is sure to be a favorite at gatherings, just like Aunt Martha makes it!

Cousin Sarah's Macaroni Salad

Ingredients:

- 2 cups elbow macaroni (or any pasta shape you prefer)
- 1 cup mayonnaise
- 2 tablespoons Dijon mustard
- 1 tablespoon apple cider vinegar
- 1 teaspoon sugar
- Salt and pepper, to taste
- 1/2 cup finely chopped red onion
- 1/2 cup diced celery
- 1/2 cup diced red bell pepper
- 1/2 cup diced cucumber
- 1/4 cup chopped fresh parsley (optional)
- 1/4 cup chopped green onions (optional)
- 1/2 cup diced ham or cooked bacon (optional)
- 1/2 cup shredded cheddar cheese (optional)

Instructions:

1. Cook the elbow macaroni according to package instructions in salted boiling water until al dente. Drain and rinse under cold water to cool completely. Drain well and transfer to a large mixing bowl.
2. In a small bowl, whisk together the mayonnaise, Dijon mustard, apple cider vinegar, sugar, salt, and pepper until well combined.
3. Pour the dressing over the cooked and cooled macaroni. Stir gently to coat the pasta evenly with the dressing.
4. Add the chopped red onion, celery, red bell pepper, cucumber, parsley, and green onions (if using). Toss gently to combine.
5. If desired, add diced ham or cooked bacon for extra flavor, and shredded cheddar cheese for creaminess.
6. Cover the macaroni salad and refrigerate for at least 1 hour before serving to allow the flavors to meld together.
7. Before serving, give the salad a gentle stir and adjust seasoning if needed with salt and pepper.
8. Serve Cousin Sarah's Macaroni Salad chilled as a side dish or light main course for your family gathering.

This macaroni salad is sure to be a hit, with its creamy dressing and fresh, crunchy vegetables. Enjoy sharing this dish with your loved ones!

Uncle Joe's BBQ Ribs

Ingredients:

- 2 racks of pork baby back ribs (about 4-5 pounds total)
- Salt and pepper, to taste

For the Dry Rub:

- 2 tablespoons brown sugar
- 1 tablespoon paprika
- 1 tablespoon garlic powder
- 1 tablespoon onion powder
- 1 teaspoon chili powder
- 1 teaspoon cumin
- 1 teaspoon salt
- 1/2 teaspoon black pepper

For the BBQ Sauce:

- 1 cup ketchup
- 1/2 cup apple cider vinegar
- 1/4 cup brown sugar
- 2 tablespoons Worcestershire sauce
- 1 tablespoon Dijon mustard
- 1 teaspoon garlic powder
- 1/2 teaspoon smoked paprika
- Salt and pepper, to taste

Instructions:

1. Preheat your oven to 300°F (150°C).
2. Remove the thin membrane from the back of the ribs. This can be done by sliding a butter knife under the membrane and then using a paper towel to grip and peel it off.
3. Season the ribs generously with salt and pepper on both sides.
4. In a small bowl, mix together all the ingredients for the dry rub: brown sugar, paprika, garlic powder, onion powder, chili powder, cumin, salt, and pepper.
5. Rub the dry rub all over the ribs, covering them evenly on both sides.
6. Wrap each rack of ribs tightly in aluminum foil, creating a packet. Place them on a baking sheet.

7. Bake the ribs in the preheated oven for 2.5 to 3 hours, or until the meat is tender and starts to pull away from the bones.
8. While the ribs are baking, prepare the BBQ sauce. In a saucepan over medium heat, combine ketchup, apple cider vinegar, brown sugar, Worcestershire sauce, Dijon mustard, garlic powder, smoked paprika, salt, and pepper. Bring to a simmer and cook for 10-15 minutes, stirring occasionally, until the sauce thickens slightly.
9. Preheat your grill to medium-high heat.
10. Carefully unwrap the foil from the ribs and discard the foil. Brush the ribs generously with the BBQ sauce on both sides.
11. Place the ribs on the preheated grill and cook for 3-4 minutes per side, or until the sauce is caramelized and the ribs have nice grill marks. Brush with additional BBQ sauce as desired while grilling.
12. Remove the ribs from the grill and let them rest for a few minutes before slicing between the bones.
13. Serve Uncle Joe's BBQ Ribs hot with extra BBQ sauce on the side and enjoy the delicious, tender ribs with your family and friends!

These BBQ ribs are sure to be a hit at your gathering, just like Uncle Joe's special recipe!

Sister Emily's Chocolate Chip Cookies

Ingredients:

- 1 cup (2 sticks) unsalted butter, softened
- 3/4 cup granulated sugar
- 3/4 cup packed light brown sugar
- 1 teaspoon vanilla extract
- 2 large eggs
- 2 1/4 cups all-purpose flour
- 1 teaspoon baking soda
- 1/2 teaspoon salt
- 2 cups semisweet chocolate chips
- 1 cup chopped nuts (optional)

Instructions:

1. Preheat your oven to 375°F (190°C). Line baking sheets with parchment paper or silicone baking mats.
2. In a large mixing bowl, cream together the softened butter, granulated sugar, brown sugar, and vanilla extract until light and fluffy.
3. Add the eggs one at a time, beating well after each addition.
4. In a separate bowl, whisk together the flour, baking soda, and salt.
5. Gradually add the dry ingredients to the creamed mixture, mixing until well combined.
6. Stir in the chocolate chips and chopped nuts (if using), ensuring they are evenly distributed throughout the cookie dough.
7. Drop rounded tablespoons of dough onto the prepared baking sheets, spacing them about 2 inches apart.
8. Bake in preheated oven for 9-11 minutes, or until the edges are lightly golden. The centers may still look slightly soft.
9. Remove from the oven and let the cookies cool on the baking sheets for 2-3 minutes before transferring them to wire racks to cool completely.
10. Enjoy Sister Emily's Chocolate Chip Cookies warm or at room temperature with a glass of milk or your favorite beverage.

These cookies will surely be a hit at any gathering, with their chewy centers, crispy edges, and generous amount of chocolate chips. Sister Emily's recipe is a timeless favorite!

Brother Mike's Buffalo Wings

Ingredients:

- 2-3 pounds chicken wings, separated into drumettes and flats
- Salt and pepper, to taste
- 1 cup all-purpose flour
- 1 teaspoon paprika
- 1 teaspoon garlic powder
- 1/2 teaspoon cayenne pepper (adjust to taste for spiciness)
- Vegetable oil, for frying

For the Buffalo Sauce:

- 1/2 cup hot sauce (such as Frank's RedHot)
- 1/2 cup unsalted butter, melted
- 1 tablespoon honey (optional, for a touch of sweetness)
- 1 teaspoon Worcestershire sauce
- 1/2 teaspoon garlic powder
- 1/2 teaspoon onion powder
- Salt and pepper, to taste

Instructions:

1. Pat dry the chicken wings with paper towels. Season with salt and pepper to taste.
2. In a large bowl, combine the flour, paprika, garlic powder, and cayenne pepper. Dredge the chicken wings in the seasoned flour mixture, shaking off any excess.
3. Heat vegetable oil in a large deep skillet or Dutch oven to 350°F (175°C) for frying. Fry the chicken wings in batches for about 10-12 minutes, or until they are golden brown and cooked through. Drain on a wire rack or paper towels.
4. In a separate bowl, whisk together the hot sauce, melted butter, honey (if using), Worcestershire sauce, garlic powder, onion powder, salt, and pepper to make the Buffalo sauce.
5. Toss the fried chicken wings in the Buffalo sauce until evenly coated. You can adjust the amount of sauce according to your preference.
6. Serve Brother Mike's Buffalo Wings hot, accompanied by celery sticks and blue cheese or ranch dressing for dipping.

Enjoy these crispy, spicy Buffalo wings as a delicious appetizer or main dish at your next gathering, just like Brother Mike makes them!

Grandma's Apple Pie

Ingredients:

For the Pie Crust:

- 2 1/2 cups all-purpose flour
- 1 cup (2 sticks) unsalted butter, chilled and cut into small cubes
- 1 teaspoon salt
- 1 tablespoon granulated sugar
- 6-8 tablespoons ice water

For the Filling:

- 6-7 cups peeled, cored, and thinly sliced apples (use a mix of tart and sweet varieties like Granny Smith and Honeycrisp)
- 1/2 cup granulated sugar
- 1/4 cup packed light brown sugar
- 1 teaspoon ground cinnamon
- 1/4 teaspoon ground nutmeg
- 1/4 teaspoon ground allspice
- 1/4 teaspoon salt
- 1 tablespoon lemon juice
- 2 tablespoons unsalted butter, cut into small pieces
- 1 tablespoon milk or cream (for brushing the crust)
- 1 tablespoon granulated sugar (for sprinkling on top)

Instructions:

For the Pie Crust:

1. In a large mixing bowl, whisk together the flour, salt, and sugar.
2. Add the chilled butter cubes to the flour mixture. Using a pastry cutter or your fingertips, work the butter into the flour until the mixture resembles coarse crumbs with some larger pea-sized pieces of butter.
3. Gradually add the ice water, 1 tablespoon at a time, mixing with a fork or your hands, until the dough begins to come together. Be careful not to overwork the dough.
4. Divide the dough into two equal portions and shape each portion into a flat disk. Wrap each disk tightly in plastic wrap and refrigerate for at least 1 hour, or overnight.

For the Filling:

1. In a large bowl, toss together the sliced apples, granulated sugar, brown sugar, cinnamon, nutmeg, allspice, salt, and lemon juice until the apples are evenly coated. Let the mixture sit for about 15-20 minutes to allow the flavors to meld.

Assembly and Baking:

1. Preheat your oven to 400°F (200°C). Place a baking sheet lined with parchment paper or aluminum foil on the bottom rack of the oven to catch any drips.
2. On a lightly floured surface, roll out one disk of the chilled pie dough into a circle about 12 inches in diameter. Carefully transfer the rolled-out dough to a 9-inch pie dish, gently pressing it into the bottom and sides of the dish. Trim any excess dough hanging over the edges with a sharp knife or kitchen shears.
3. Spoon the apple filling into the prepared pie crust, spreading it out evenly. Dot the top of the filling with the pieces of unsalted butter.
4. Roll out the second disk of chilled pie dough into a circle about 12 inches in diameter. Place the rolled-out dough over the filling. Trim any excess dough hanging over the edges, leaving about a 1-inch overhang. Fold the overhang under itself and crimp the edges to seal. Cut a few small slits in the top crust to allow steam to escape during baking.
5. Brush the top crust with milk or cream and sprinkle evenly with granulated sugar.
6. Place the pie on the preheated baking sheet in the oven. Bake for 45-55 minutes, or until the crust is golden brown and the filling is bubbly.
7. If the edges of the crust start to brown too quickly, cover them loosely with foil or a pie shield.
8. Remove the pie from the oven and let it cool on a wire rack for at least 2 hours before slicing and serving.

Enjoy Grandma's Apple Pie warm or at room temperature, optionally topped with vanilla ice cream or whipped cream. This recipe is sure to bring back fond memories of homemade goodness!

Mom's Chicken Parmesan

Ingredients:

- 4 boneless, skinless chicken breasts
- Salt and pepper, to taste
- 1 cup all-purpose flour
- 2 large eggs, beaten
- 1 cup Italian-style breadcrumbs
- 1/2 cup grated Parmesan cheese
- 1/2 teaspoon dried oregano
- 1/2 teaspoon dried basil
- 1/2 teaspoon garlic powder
- 1/4 cup olive oil, for frying
- 2 cups marinara sauce (homemade or store-bought)
- 1 cup shredded mozzarella cheese
- Fresh basil or parsley, chopped (for garnish)

Instructions:

1. Preheat your oven to 375°F (190°C).
2. Place each chicken breast between two sheets of plastic wrap or wax paper. Using a meat mallet or rolling pin, pound the chicken to an even thickness of about 1/2 inch. Season both sides of the chicken breasts with salt and pepper.
3. Set up a breading station: In one shallow bowl, place the flour. In another shallow bowl, beat the eggs. In a third shallow bowl, combine the breadcrumbs, grated Parmesan cheese, dried oregano, dried basil, and garlic powder.
4. Dredge each chicken breast in the flour, shaking off any excess. Dip into the beaten eggs, allowing any excess to drip off. Finally, coat the chicken breasts evenly with the breadcrumb mixture, pressing gently to adhere.
5. In a large oven-safe skillet or baking dish, heat the olive oil over medium-high heat. Add the breaded chicken breasts and cook for about 3-4 minutes per side, or until golden brown and cooked through. You may need to cook them in batches to avoid overcrowding the pan.
6. Remove the cooked chicken breasts from the skillet and place them on a plate lined with paper towels to drain excess oil.
7. Pour marinara sauce into the skillet or baking dish, spreading it evenly. Place the cooked chicken breasts on top of the marinara sauce.
8. Sprinkle shredded mozzarella cheese evenly over each chicken breast.

9. Transfer the skillet or baking dish to the preheated oven and bake for 20-25 minutes, or until the cheese is melted and bubbly.
10. Remove from the oven and let the Chicken Parmesan rest for a few minutes. Garnish with chopped fresh basil or parsley before serving.
11. Serve Mom's Chicken Parmesan hot, alongside pasta, garlic bread, or a fresh green salad.

Enjoy this comforting and flavorful Chicken Parmesan recipe that's sure to be a hit with your family, just like Mom makes it!

Dad's Steak and Potatoes

Ingredients:

For the Steak:

- 4 (8-ounce) beef steaks (such as ribeye, sirloin, or New York strip)
- Salt and pepper, to taste
- 2 tablespoons olive oil
- 2 cloves garlic, minced
- 2 tablespoons fresh rosemary or thyme, chopped (optional)
- 2 tablespoons butter

For the Potatoes:

- 4 large potatoes (such as Russet or Yukon Gold), scrubbed and dried
- 2 tablespoons olive oil
- Salt and pepper, to taste
- 1 teaspoon garlic powder
- 1 teaspoon paprika
- Fresh parsley, chopped (for garnish)

Instructions:

For the Steak:

1. Remove the steaks from the refrigerator and let them come to room temperature, about 30 minutes to 1 hour before cooking. Season both sides of each steak generously with salt and pepper.
2. In a large skillet or cast iron pan, heat olive oil over medium-high heat until hot but not smoking.
3. Add the steaks to the skillet and sear for about 4-5 minutes on each side, or until they reach your desired level of doneness (use a meat thermometer to check: 125°F (52°C) for rare, 135°F (57°C) for medium rare, 145°F (63°C) for medium, 160°F (71°C) for medium well, or 165°F (74°C) for well done).
4. During the last minute of cooking, add minced garlic, fresh herbs (if using), and butter to the skillet. Baste the steaks with the melted butter and herbs, continuously spooning the mixture over the steaks.
5. Remove the steaks from the skillet and let them rest on a cutting board for 5-10 minutes before slicing.

For the Potatoes:

1. Preheat your oven to 400°F (200°C).
2. Cut the potatoes into 1-inch cubes or wedges. Place them on a large baking sheet.
3. Drizzle olive oil over the potatoes and toss to coat evenly. Season with salt, pepper, garlic powder, and paprika, tossing again to distribute the seasonings.
4. Arrange the potatoes in a single layer on the baking sheet.
5. Roast in the preheated oven for 30-35 minutes, or until the potatoes are golden brown and crispy on the outside, and tender on the inside. Stir the potatoes halfway through cooking for even browning.

Assembly:

1. Serve Dad's Steak and Potatoes hot, with the sliced steak arranged on a plate alongside the roasted potatoes.
2. Garnish with chopped fresh parsley for added freshness and color.
3. Enjoy this hearty and delicious meal with your family, just like Dad makes it!

This recipe will surely satisfy everyone's appetite with tender steak and flavorful roasted potatoes.

Aunt Martha's Tuna Casserole

Ingredients:

- 8 ounces egg noodles (or pasta of your choice)
- 2 tablespoons butter
- 1 small onion, finely chopped
- 2 cloves garlic, minced
- 1 cup sliced mushrooms (optional)
- 1/4 cup all-purpose flour
- 2 cups milk
- 1 cup chicken or vegetable broth
- 1 teaspoon Dijon mustard
- 1/2 teaspoon salt, or to taste
- 1/4 teaspoon black pepper, or to taste
- 1/4 teaspoon dried thyme (optional)
- 2 (5-ounce) cans tuna, drained and flaked
- 1 cup frozen peas, thawed
- 1 cup shredded cheddar cheese
- 1/2 cup breadcrumbs
- 2 tablespoons grated Parmesan cheese
- Fresh parsley, chopped (for garnish)

Instructions:

1. Preheat your oven to 375°F (190°C). Grease a 9x13 inch baking dish or a similar-sized casserole dish.
2. Cook the egg noodles (or pasta) according to package instructions until al dente. Drain and set aside.
3. In a large skillet or saucepan, melt the butter over medium heat. Add the chopped onion and sauté until softened, about 3-4 minutes. Add the minced garlic and sliced mushrooms (if using), and cook for an additional 2-3 minutes until mushrooms are tender.
4. Sprinkle the flour over the onion and mushrooms. Cook, stirring constantly, for 1-2 minutes to cook off the raw flour taste.
5. Gradually whisk in the milk and chicken or vegetable broth, stirring constantly to prevent lumps from forming. Cook until the mixture thickens and comes to a simmer, about 5-7 minutes.
6. Stir in the Dijon mustard, salt, black pepper, and dried thyme (if using). Remove from heat.

7. In a large mixing bowl, combine the cooked egg noodles, flaked tuna, thawed peas, and shredded cheddar cheese. Pour the sauce over the noodle mixture and gently toss to combine.
8. Transfer the mixture to the greased baking dish, spreading it out evenly.
9. In a small bowl, combine the breadcrumbs and grated Parmesan cheese. Sprinkle this mixture evenly over the top of the casserole.
10. Bake in the preheated oven for 25-30 minutes, or until the casserole is bubbly and the breadcrumbs are golden brown.
11. Remove from the oven and let it cool for a few minutes before serving.
12. Garnish Aunt Martha's Tuna Casserole with chopped fresh parsley before serving. Enjoy this comforting dish with your family!

This tuna casserole recipe combines creamy sauce, tender pasta, flavorful tuna, and wholesome vegetables, making it a perfect choice for a cozy family meal, just like Aunt Martha used to make!

Cousin Sarah's Cornbread

Ingredients:

- 1 cup yellow cornmeal
- 1 cup all-purpose flour
- 1/4 cup granulated sugar (adjust to taste)
- 1 tablespoon baking powder
- 1/2 teaspoon baking soda
- 1/2 teaspoon salt
- 1 cup buttermilk
- 1/2 cup unsalted butter, melted and cooled slightly
- 2 large eggs
- 1 cup corn kernels (fresh, canned, or thawed if frozen)
- Optional: 1/2 cup shredded cheddar cheese, chopped jalapeños, or diced green chilies for added flavor (optional)

Instructions:

1. Preheat your oven to 375°F (190°C). Grease a 9x9 inch baking dish or a similar-sized baking pan.
2. In a large bowl, whisk together the cornmeal, flour, sugar, baking powder, baking soda, and salt until well combined.
3. In another bowl, whisk together the buttermilk, melted butter, and eggs until smooth.
4. Pour the wet ingredients into the dry ingredients and stir until just combined. Do not overmix; it's okay if there are a few lumps.
5. Gently fold in the corn kernels and any optional ingredients like shredded cheese or jalapeños.
6. Pour the batter into the prepared baking dish, spreading it out evenly.
7. Bake in the preheated oven for 25-30 minutes, or until the top is golden brown and a toothpick inserted into the center comes out clean.
8. Remove from the oven and let Cousin Sarah's Cornbread cool in the pan for about 10 minutes before slicing and serving.
9. Serve warm as a side dish with chili, BBQ, soups, or enjoy it on its own with butter and honey.

This cornbread recipe is sure to be a hit at family gatherings, with its tender crumb and sweet corn flavor. Enjoy sharing Cousin Sarah's Cornbread with your loved ones!

Uncle Joe's Pulled Pork Sandwiches

Ingredients:

For the Pulled Pork:

- 3-4 pounds pork shoulder (also known as pork butt), boneless
- Salt and pepper, to taste
- 2 tablespoons brown sugar
- 1 tablespoon paprika
- 1 tablespoon garlic powder
- 1 tablespoon onion powder
- 1 teaspoon cumin
- 1 teaspoon chili powder
- 1/2 teaspoon cayenne pepper (adjust to taste for spiciness)
- 1 cup chicken broth or water
- 1/2 cup apple cider vinegar
- 1/4 cup barbecue sauce (plus more for serving)
- 2 tablespoons Worcestershire sauce
- 1 tablespoon liquid smoke (optional)

For Serving:

- Hamburger buns or sandwich rolls
- Coleslaw (optional, for topping)

Instructions:

1. Preheat your oven to 300°F (150°C).
2. Pat dry the pork shoulder with paper towels. Season all sides generously with salt and pepper.
3. In a small bowl, combine brown sugar, paprika, garlic powder, onion powder, cumin, chili powder, and cayenne pepper.
4. Rub the spice mixture evenly all over the pork shoulder, covering it completely.
5. In a roasting pan or Dutch oven, combine chicken broth (or water) and apple cider vinegar. Place the seasoned pork shoulder into the pan.
6. Cover the roasting pan tightly with aluminum foil or a lid. Roast in the preheated oven for 4-5 hours, or until the pork is very tender and easily pulls apart with a fork.
7. Remove the pork shoulder from the oven and transfer it to a cutting board. Let it rest for 10-15 minutes.

8. Using two forks, shred the pork into bite-sized pieces. Discard any large pieces of fat.
9. In a saucepan or skillet, combine shredded pork with barbecue sauce, Worcestershire sauce, and liquid smoke (if using). Heat over medium heat until warmed through, stirring occasionally.
10. To assemble the sandwiches, toast the hamburger buns or sandwich rolls if desired. Place a generous portion of pulled pork onto the bottom half of each bun.
11. Top with coleslaw if desired, and drizzle with additional barbecue sauce.
12. Cover with the top half of the bun and serve Uncle Joe's Pulled Pork Sandwiches immediately.

Enjoy these flavorful pulled pork sandwiches at your next gathering, just like Uncle Joe makes them! They're perfect for feeding a crowd and always a hit with friends and family.

Sister Emily's Brownies

Ingredients:

- 1 cup (2 sticks) unsalted butter
- 2 cups granulated sugar
- 4 large eggs
- 2 teaspoons vanilla extract
- 1 cup all-purpose flour
- 3/4 cup unsweetened cocoa powder
- 1/2 teaspoon salt
- 1 cup semi-sweet chocolate chips (optional)
- 1 cup chopped nuts (optional)

Instructions:

1. Preheat your oven to 350°F (175°C). Grease a 9x13 inch baking pan or line it with parchment paper.
2. In a medium saucepan, melt the butter over medium heat. Remove from heat and stir in sugar until well combined.
3. Add the eggs one at a time, stirring well after each addition.
4. Stir in vanilla extract.
5. In a separate bowl, whisk together flour, cocoa powder, and salt.
6. Gradually add the flour mixture to the butter mixture, stirring until just combined.
7. If using, fold in chocolate chips and chopped nuts until evenly distributed in the batter.
8. Pour the batter into the prepared baking pan and spread it out evenly with a spatula.
9. Bake in the preheated oven for 25-30 minutes, or until a toothpick inserted into the center comes out with moist crumbs (not wet batter).
10. Remove from the oven and let Sister Emily's Brownies cool completely in the pan on a wire rack.
11. Once cooled, cut into squares and serve. Optionally, dust with powdered sugar or drizzle with melted chocolate for extra indulgence.

These brownies are perfect for any occasion, whether it's a family gathering, potluck, or just a sweet treat to enjoy with a glass of milk or coffee. Sister Emily's recipe ensures they're moist, chocolatey, and absolutely irresistible!

Brother Mike's Guacamole

Ingredients:

- 3 ripe avocados
- 1 lime, juiced
- 1/2 teaspoon salt, or to taste
- 1/2 teaspoon ground cumin
- 1/2 teaspoon chili powder
- 1/4 teaspoon cayenne pepper (optional, for extra heat)
- 1/2 cup red onion, finely diced
- 1/2 cup tomato, diced and seeds removed
- 1/4 cup fresh cilantro, chopped
- 1-2 cloves garlic, minced
- Optional: 1 jalapeño pepper, seeded and minced (for extra spice)
- Optional: 1/2 teaspoon ground coriander
- Optional: 1/2 teaspoon smoked paprika

Instructions:

1. Cut the avocados in half, remove the pits, and scoop the flesh into a medium bowl.
2. Mash the avocado with a fork or potato masher until it reaches your desired consistency (smooth or chunky).
3. Add lime juice, salt, ground cumin, chili powder, and cayenne pepper (if using). Mix well to combine.
4. Fold in diced red onion, diced tomato, chopped cilantro, minced garlic, and jalapeño (if using).
5. Taste and adjust seasoning as needed, adding more salt or lime juice if desired.
6. For additional flavor, you can also add ground coriander and smoked paprika, mixing until evenly incorporated.
7. Cover the guacamole with plastic wrap, pressing it directly onto the surface to prevent browning, and refrigerate for at least 30 minutes to let the flavors meld.
8. Before serving, give Brother Mike's Guacamole a quick stir and adjust seasoning if necessary.
9. Serve with tortilla chips, as a topping for tacos or nachos, or alongside grilled meats and vegetables.

Brother Mike's guacamole is sure to be a hit with its fresh ingredients and bold flavors. Enjoy sharing this delicious dip with family and friends!

Grandma's Chicken Soup

Ingredients:

- 1 whole chicken (about 3-4 lbs), cut into pieces
- 10 cups water (or chicken broth)
- 3 carrots, peeled and sliced
- 3 celery stalks, sliced
- 1 onion, diced
- 2 cloves garlic, minced
- 1 bay leaf
- 1 teaspoon dried thyme
- 1 teaspoon dried parsley
- Salt and pepper to taste
- 1 cup egg noodles or rice (optional)
- Fresh parsley, chopped (for garnish)

Instructions:

1. Prepare the Chicken: In a large pot, place the chicken pieces and cover with water (or chicken broth). Bring to a boil over medium-high heat. Skim off any foam that rises to the top. Reduce heat to low and simmer, partially covered, for about 1 hour until the chicken is cooked through and tender.
2. Remove Chicken and Strain Broth: Once the chicken is cooked, remove it from the pot and set aside to cool. Strain the broth through a fine mesh sieve to remove any impurities. Discard any solids.
3. Prepare Soup Base: Return the strained broth to the pot. Add carrots, celery, onion, garlic, bay leaf, dried thyme, dried parsley, salt, and pepper. Bring to a boil, then reduce heat and simmer for about 20 minutes until the vegetables are tender.
4. Shred Chicken: While the vegetables are cooking, shred the cooled chicken meat, discarding bones and skin.
5. Add Chicken and Noodles/Rice: Once the vegetables are tender, add the shredded chicken back into the pot. If using, add egg noodles or rice. Cook for an additional 10-15 minutes until the noodles/rice are tender.
6. Adjust Seasoning and Serve: Taste and adjust seasoning with more salt and pepper if needed. Remove the bay leaf before serving. Garnish with chopped fresh parsley.
7. Serve: Ladle the warm Grandma's Chicken Soup into bowls and serve hot. Enjoy the comforting flavors!

This recipe yields a hearty and flavorful chicken soup that's perfect for warming up on a chilly day or for soothing a cold. Feel free to adjust the ingredients and seasonings to suit your taste preferences or family traditions!

Mom's Spaghetti and Meatballs

Ingredients:

For the Meatballs:

- 1 lb ground beef (or a mix of beef and pork)
- 1/2 cup breadcrumbs
- 1/4 cup grated Parmesan cheese
- 1/4 cup milk
- 1 egg
- 2 cloves garlic, minced
- 1 tablespoon fresh parsley, chopped
- 1 teaspoon dried oregano
- 1/2 teaspoon salt
- 1/4 teaspoon black pepper

For the Sauce:

- 2 tablespoons olive oil
- 1 onion, finely chopped
- 3 cloves garlic, minced
- 1 can (28 oz) crushed tomatoes
- 1 can (14 oz) diced tomatoes
- 2 tablespoons tomato paste
- 1 teaspoon dried basil
- 1 teaspoon dried oregano
- 1/2 teaspoon sugar (optional, to balance acidity)
- Salt and pepper to taste

For the Pasta:

- 1 lb spaghetti or pasta of your choice
- Salt for boiling water

Instructions:

1. Make the Meatballs:

- In a large bowl, combine ground beef, breadcrumbs, Parmesan cheese, milk, egg, minced garlic, parsley, dried oregano, salt, and pepper. Mix until well combined.
- Shape the mixture into meatballs, about 1-1.5 inches in diameter.

2. Cook the Meatballs:

- Heat olive oil in a large skillet over medium heat. Add the meatballs in batches and cook until browned on all sides, about 6-8 minutes. Remove meatballs from skillet and set aside.

3. Prepare the Sauce:

- In the same skillet, add a bit more olive oil if needed. Saute the chopped onion until softened, about 5 minutes. Add minced garlic and cook for another 1-2 minutes until fragrant.
- Stir in crushed tomatoes, diced tomatoes (with their juices), tomato paste, dried basil, dried oregano, sugar (if using), salt, and pepper. Bring to a simmer.

4. Simmer the Sauce:

- Return the meatballs to the skillet with the sauce. Cover and simmer over low heat for 30-40 minutes, stirring occasionally, until meatballs are cooked through and sauce is flavorful. Adjust seasoning if needed.

5. Cook the Pasta:

- While the sauce is simmering, cook the spaghetti according to package instructions in a large pot of salted boiling water until al dente. Drain well.

6. Serve:

- Serve Mom's Spaghetti and Meatballs by placing a portion of spaghetti onto each plate or bowl. Top with meatballs and sauce. Garnish with additional Parmesan cheese and fresh chopped parsley if desired.

7. Enjoy:

- Serve hot and enjoy this comforting and delicious dish with family and friends!

This recipe captures the essence of a homemade spaghetti and meatballs dish that's sure to bring back memories of home-cooked meals. Adjust the ingredients and seasonings to suit your taste preferences and make it your own!

Dad's Chili

Ingredients:

- 1 lb ground beef (or turkey, chicken, or a mix)
- 1 onion, chopped
- 3 cloves garlic, minced
- 1 bell pepper (any color), chopped
- 1 can (15 oz) kidney beans, drained and rinsed
- 1 can (15 oz) black beans, drained and rinsed
- 1 can (15 oz) diced tomatoes
- 1 can (6 oz) tomato paste
- 2 cups beef broth (or chicken broth)
- 1 tablespoon chili powder
- 1 teaspoon ground cumin
- 1 teaspoon paprika
- 1/2 teaspoon dried oregano
- 1/2 teaspoon cayenne pepper (optional, for heat)
- Salt and pepper to taste
- Olive oil, for cooking
- Optional toppings: shredded cheese, sour cream, chopped green onions, cilantro, diced avocado

Instructions:

1. Brown the Meat: In a large pot or Dutch oven, heat a drizzle of olive oil over medium-high heat. Add the ground beef and cook, breaking it apart with a spoon, until browned and cooked through. Drain excess fat if needed.
2. Saute Aromatics: Add chopped onion, minced garlic, and bell pepper to the pot with the cooked meat. Saute for 5-7 minutes, until vegetables are softened.
3. Add Beans and Tomatoes: Stir in kidney beans, black beans, diced tomatoes (with their juices), and tomato paste. Mix well to combine.
4. Season: Add chili powder, ground cumin, paprika, dried oregano, cayenne pepper (if using), salt, and pepper to taste. Stir to combine all ingredients.
5. Simmer: Pour in beef broth (or chicken broth) to the pot. Bring the chili to a boil, then reduce heat to low. Cover and simmer for at least 30 minutes to allow the flavors to meld together. Stir occasionally.
6. Adjust Consistency and Seasoning: If the chili is too thick, you can add more broth or water to reach your desired consistency. Taste and adjust seasoning if needed, adding more chili powder, cumin, or salt and pepper to taste.

7. Serve: Ladle Dad's Chili into bowls and serve hot. Garnish with shredded cheese, a dollop of sour cream, chopped green onions, cilantro, or diced avocado if desired.
8. Enjoy: Enjoy this hearty and comforting Dad's Chili with your favorite toppings and perhaps some cornbread or tortilla chips on the side.

This recipe is versatile, so feel free to adjust the ingredients and seasonings to suit your taste preferences. Dad's Chili is perfect for feeding a crowd or for leftovers that taste even better the next day!

Aunt Martha's Beef Stew

Ingredients:

- 2 lbs stew beef, cut into 1-inch cubes
- 3 tablespoons all-purpose flour
- Salt and pepper to taste
- 2 tablespoons olive oil
- 1 onion, diced
- 3 cloves garlic, minced
- 4 cups beef broth
- 1 cup red wine (optional, can substitute with more broth)
- 2 tablespoons tomato paste
- 2 bay leaves
- 1 teaspoon dried thyme
- 1 teaspoon dried rosemary
- 1 lb potatoes, peeled and cut into chunks
- 3 carrots, peeled and sliced
- 2 celery stalks, sliced
- 1 cup frozen peas (optional)
- Chopped fresh parsley, for garnish

Instructions:

1. Prepare the Beef:
    - In a bowl, season the stew beef with salt and pepper. Sprinkle with flour and toss to coat evenly.
2. Brown the Beef:
    - In a large Dutch oven or heavy pot, heat olive oil over medium-high heat. Add the beef cubes in batches and brown them on all sides. Remove the browned beef cubes and set aside.
3. Saute Aromatics:
    - In the same pot, add diced onion and minced garlic. Cook for 3-4 minutes until softened and fragrant.
4. Deglaze the Pot:
    - Pour in the beef broth and red wine (if using), scraping the bottom of the pot to loosen any browned bits (this adds flavor). Stir in tomato paste, bay leaves, dried thyme, and dried rosemary.
5. Simmer the Stew:

- Return the browned beef cubes to the pot. Bring the mixture to a boil, then reduce heat to low. Cover and simmer for 1.5 to 2 hours, stirring occasionally, until the beef is tender.
6. **Add Vegetables:**
    - Add potatoes, carrots, and celery to the pot. Stir to combine. Cover and simmer for an additional 30-40 minutes, or until vegetables are tender and flavors have melded.
7. **Add Peas (if using):**
    - If using frozen peas, add them to the stew during the last 5-10 minutes of cooking, until heated through.
8. **Adjust Seasoning and Serve:**
    - Taste and adjust seasoning with salt and pepper if needed. Remove bay leaves before serving.
9. **Serve:**
    - Ladle Aunt Martha's Beef Stew into bowls. Garnish with chopped fresh parsley for a pop of color and freshness.
10. **Enjoy:**
- Enjoy this comforting and hearty beef stew with crusty bread or over mashed potatoes for a delicious meal that will warm you up from the inside out.

This recipe captures the essence of a homemade beef stew, perfect for family dinners or gatherings during cooler weather. Adjust the ingredients and seasonings according to your preferences, and savor each spoonful of Aunt Martha's comforting creation!

Cousin Sarah's Caesar Salad

Ingredients:

For the Salad:

- 1 head of romaine lettuce, washed and chopped
- 1 cup croutons (homemade or store-bought)
- 1/4 cup shaved or grated Parmesan cheese

For the Dressing:

- 1/2 cup mayonnaise
- 1/4 cup grated Parmesan cheese
- 2 tablespoons lemon juice (about 1 lemon)
- 1 tablespoon Dijon mustard
- 1 clove garlic, minced
- 1/2 teaspoon Worcestershire sauce
- Salt and pepper to taste
- Optional: anchovy paste (about 1 teaspoon, or to taste)

Instructions:

1. Prepare the Dressing:
    - In a small bowl, whisk together mayonnaise, grated Parmesan cheese, lemon juice, Dijon mustard, minced garlic, Worcestershire sauce, salt, and pepper. If using anchovy paste, add it to the dressing and whisk until smooth. Adjust seasoning to taste.
2. Assemble the Salad:
    - In a large salad bowl, add chopped romaine lettuce.
3. Add Croutons and Parmesan:
    - Sprinkle croutons over the lettuce. Add shaved or grated Parmesan cheese on top.
4. Toss with Dressing:
    - Pour desired amount of Caesar dressing over the salad (you may not need all of it; start with half and add more as needed). Use salad tongs or two large spoons to gently toss the salad until evenly coated with dressing.
5. Serve:
    - Divide Cousin Sarah's Caesar Salad into individual bowls or plates.
6. Optional Additions:

- For a heartier salad, you can add grilled chicken breast slices, cooked shrimp, or crispy bacon strips.
7. Enjoy:
    - Serve immediately and enjoy this fresh and flavorful Cousin Sarah's Caesar Salad as a side dish or a light meal!

This recipe provides a creamy and tangy Caesar dressing that complements the crisp romaine lettuce and crunchy croutons perfectly. It's a versatile dish that you can adjust to your taste preferences and enjoy any time of the year!

Uncle Joe's Baked Beans

Ingredients:

- 1 lb dried navy beans (or any small white beans)
- 1 onion, finely chopped
- 1/2 lb bacon, chopped
- 1/2 cup molasses
- 1/4 cup brown sugar
- 1/4 cup ketchup
- 2 tablespoons mustard (yellow or Dijon)
- 1 teaspoon Worcestershire sauce
- 1 teaspoon salt
- 1/2 teaspoon black pepper
- 4 cups water (for soaking beans)
- 4 cups chicken or vegetable broth (for cooking beans)

Instructions:

1. Prepare the Beans:
    - Rinse the dried beans under cold water and remove any debris. Place them in a large bowl and cover with about 4 cups of water. Let the beans soak overnight (at least 8 hours). Alternatively, you can use the quick soak method: Bring the beans and water to a boil, remove from heat, cover, and let sit for 1 hour. Drain and rinse.
2. Preheat the Oven:
    - Preheat your oven to 325°F (160°C).
3. Cook the Bacon and Onion:
    - In a large oven-safe pot or Dutch oven, cook the chopped bacon over medium heat until it starts to render fat. Add the finely chopped onion and cook together until the onion is softened and bacon is cooked, about 5-7 minutes.
4. Combine Ingredients:
    - To the pot with bacon and onion, add molasses, brown sugar, ketchup, mustard, Worcestershire sauce, salt, and black pepper. Stir to combine well.
5. Add Beans and Liquid:
    - Add the soaked and drained beans to the pot. Pour in enough chicken or vegetable broth to cover the beans by about 1 inch. Stir everything together.

6. Bake the Beans:
    - Cover the pot with a lid or aluminum foil and transfer to the preheated oven. Bake for 3-4 hours, stirring occasionally, until the beans are tender and the sauce has thickened. If the beans seem too dry during baking, you can add a bit more broth or water.
7. Serve:
    - Once baked, taste and adjust seasoning if needed. Serve Uncle Joe's Baked Beans hot as a side dish to grilled meats, sandwiches, or as part of a buffet-style meal.
8. Enjoy:
    - Enjoy these delicious, homemade baked beans with family and friends! They're perfect for gatherings and are sure to become a favorite comfort food.

This recipe captures the essence of classic baked beans with a rich, sweet, and savory flavor profile that's loved by many. Adjust the sweetness or spice level to your preference and savor each spoonful of Uncle Joe's flavorful creation!

Sister Emily's Banana Bread

Ingredients:

- 2 to 3 ripe bananas, mashed (about 1 cup)
- 1/2 cup unsalted butter, melted
- 3/4 cup granulated sugar
- 1 large egg, beaten
- 1 teaspoon vanilla extract
- 1 teaspoon baking soda
- 1/4 teaspoon salt
- 1 1/2 cups all-purpose flour
- Optional add-ins: 1/2 cup chopped nuts (walnuts or pecans), chocolate chips, or dried fruit

Instructions:

1. Preheat Oven and Prepare Pan:
    - Preheat your oven to 350°F (175°C). Grease a 9x5-inch loaf pan or line it with parchment paper.
2. Mash Bananas:
    - In a mixing bowl, mash the ripe bananas with a fork or potato masher until smooth.
3. Mix Wet Ingredients:
    - Stir melted butter into the mashed bananas.
4. Add Sugar, Egg, and Vanilla:
    - Mix in the sugar, beaten egg, and vanilla extract until well combined.
5. Incorporate Dry Ingredients:
    - Sprinkle the baking soda and salt over the mixture and stir to combine.
    - Gradually add the flour, stirring just until the flour is incorporated. Be careful not to overmix; a few lumps are okay.
    - If using, gently fold in chopped nuts, chocolate chips, or dried fruit until evenly distributed in the batter.
6. Pour Batter into Pan:
    - Pour the banana bread batter into the prepared loaf pan, spreading it evenly with a spatula.
7. Bake:
    - Bake in the preheated oven for 50 to 60 minutes, or until a toothpick inserted into the center comes out clean.
8. Cool and Serve:

- Allow Sister Emily's Banana Bread to cool in the pan for 10 minutes. Then, transfer it to a wire rack to cool completely before slicing.
9. Enjoy:
    - Slice and enjoy Sister Emily's Banana Bread warm or at room temperature. It's perfect for breakfast, as a snack, or as a thoughtful homemade gift!

This recipe produces a moist and flavorful banana bread that's sure to become a favorite. Feel free to customize it with your favorite mix-ins or enjoy it as is, letting the natural sweetness of ripe bananas shine through.

Brother Mike's Nachos

Ingredients:

- 1 bag (about 10-12 oz) tortilla chips
- 1 lb ground beef or turkey
- 1 packet (about 1 oz) taco seasoning mix
- 1 can (15 oz) refried beans
- 1 cup shredded cheddar cheese (or Mexican blend cheese)
- 1 cup shredded Monterey Jack cheese (or another melting cheese)
- 1/2 cup diced tomatoes
- 1/2 cup diced red onion
- 1/4 cup sliced black olives
- 1 jalapeño, sliced (optional, for heat)
- Fresh cilantro, chopped, for garnish
- Sour cream, guacamole, salsa, or your favorite toppings for serving

Instructions:

1. Preheat Oven:
    - Preheat your oven to 350°F (175°C). Line a baking sheet with parchment paper or foil for easy cleanup.
2. Cook Ground Meat:
    - In a skillet over medium-high heat, cook the ground beef or turkey until browned and cooked through. Drain any excess fat. Add the taco seasoning mix and prepare according to package instructions.
3. Warm Refried Beans:
    - In a microwave-safe bowl, heat the refried beans until warm and easy to spread.
4. Assemble Nachos:
    - Arrange half of the tortilla chips in a single layer on the prepared baking sheet. Spoon half of the warm refried beans over the chips. Sprinkle half of the cooked seasoned meat evenly over the beans.
    - Sprinkle half of each cheese evenly over the chips, beans, and meat. Repeat with another layer using the remaining chips, beans, meat, and cheese.
5. Add Toppings:
    - Sprinkle diced tomatoes, diced red onion, sliced black olives, and jalapeño slices (if using) evenly over the top of the nachos.
6. Bake:

        - Place the baking sheet in the preheated oven and bake for about 10-15 minutes, or until the cheese is melted and bubbly.
7. Garnish and Serve:
    - Remove from the oven and sprinkle chopped cilantro over the nachos. Serve Brother Mike's Nachos hot with sour cream, guacamole, salsa, or your favorite toppings.
8. Enjoy:
    - Dig into these delicious, loaded nachos with family and friends! They're perfect for game day gatherings, parties, or anytime you're craving a flavorful snack.

Feel free to customize Brother Mike's Nachos by adding additional toppings like jalapeños, bell peppers, or even cooked beans. Adjust the spice level with more or less jalapeños and enjoy this crowd-pleasing snack!

Grandma's Pancakes

Ingredients:

- 1 1/2 cups all-purpose flour
- 3 1/2 teaspoons baking powder
- 1 teaspoon salt
- 1 tablespoon white sugar
- 1 1/4 cups milk
- 1 egg
- 3 tablespoons melted butter or vegetable oil
- Butter or oil for cooking
- Optional: Maple syrup, fresh berries, sliced bananas, or other toppings

Instructions:

1. Mix Dry Ingredients:
   - In a large bowl, whisk together the flour, baking powder, salt, and sugar until well combined.
2. Prepare Wet Ingredients:
   - In another bowl, whisk together the milk, egg, and melted butter or oil.
3. Combine Wet and Dry Ingredients:
   - Pour the wet ingredients into the dry ingredients. Stir gently with a spoon or whisk until just combined. It's okay if there are a few lumps; do not overmix the batter.
4. Heat the Griddle or Pan:
   - Heat a non-stick griddle or large skillet over medium heat. Add a small amount of butter or oil and spread it evenly over the surface.
5. Cook the Pancakes:
   - For each pancake, pour about 1/4 cup of batter onto the hot griddle. Use the back of a spoon or measuring cup to spread the batter into a round shape if needed.
   - Cook until bubbles form on the surface of the pancake and the edges look set, about 2-3 minutes.
6. Flip and Cook:
   - Carefully flip the pancake with a spatula and cook until golden brown on the other side, about 1-2 minutes more.
7. Keep Warm:

- Transfer cooked pancakes to a plate and cover loosely with aluminum foil to keep warm while you cook the remaining pancakes. Repeat the cooking process with the remaining batter.

8. Serve:
    - Serve Grandma's pancakes hot with butter, maple syrup, and any other toppings you desire.
9. Enjoy:
    - Enjoy these classic, homemade pancakes that remind you of Grandma's kitchen. They're perfect for breakfast or brunch with family and friends!

Feel free to add a touch of vanilla extract or cinnamon to the batter for extra flavor, or incorporate chocolate chips or blueberries into the pancakes for a delicious variation. Customize Grandma's pancakes to your liking and savor the nostalgic taste of homemade goodness!

Mom's Quiche

Ingredients:

For the Crust:

- 1 1/4 cups all-purpose flour
- 1/2 teaspoon salt
- 1/2 cup cold unsalted butter, cut into small cubes
- 3-4 tablespoons ice water

For the Filling:

- 1 cup milk (whole milk or half-and-half)
- 4 large eggs
- 1 cup shredded cheese (cheddar, Swiss, Gruyere, or your favorite)
- 1 cup diced cooked ham, cooked bacon, or cooked vegetables (such as spinach, mushrooms, or bell peppers)
- Salt and pepper to taste
- Optional: 1/4 teaspoon dried herbs (such as thyme or parsley)

Instructions:

1. Prepare the Crust:
    - In a large bowl, whisk together the flour and salt. Add the cubed butter and use a pastry cutter or fork to cut the butter into the flour mixture until it resembles coarse crumbs.
    - Gradually add the ice water, one tablespoon at a time, mixing with a fork until the dough begins to come together. You may not need to use all the water.
    - Gather the dough into a ball, flatten it into a disk, wrap it in plastic wrap, and refrigerate for at least 30 minutes.
2. Preheat Oven:
    - Preheat your oven to 375°F (190°C).
3. Roll Out and Shape the Crust:
    - On a lightly floured surface, roll out the chilled dough into a circle about 12 inches in diameter. Carefully transfer the dough to a 9-inch pie dish. Press the dough into the bottom and up the sides of the dish. Trim any excess dough hanging over the edges. Optionally, crimp the edges of the crust with your fingers or a fork.
4. Blind Bake the Crust (optional):

- To prevent a soggy crust, you can blind bake it before adding the filling. Line the crust with parchment paper or aluminum foil and fill with pie weights or dried beans. Bake in the preheated oven for about 15 minutes. Remove the weights and parchment/foil, then bake for an additional 5 minutes until lightly golden. Remove from oven and let cool slightly.
5. Prepare the Filling:
    - In a medium bowl, whisk together the eggs and milk until well combined. Season with salt, pepper, and dried herbs if using.
6. Assemble the Quiche:
    - Spread the shredded cheese evenly over the bottom of the partially baked crust. Sprinkle the diced ham, bacon, or cooked vegetables over the cheese.
7. Pour in the Egg Mixture:
    - Carefully pour the egg and milk mixture over the cheese and fillings in the crust.
8. Bake the Quiche:
    - Place the quiche in the preheated oven and bake for 30-35 minutes, or until the quiche is set and the top is lightly golden brown.
9. Cool and Serve:
    - Remove the quiche from the oven and let it cool in the pie dish for about 10 minutes before slicing and serving.
10. Enjoy:
- Serve Mom's quiche warm or at room temperature, accompanied by a fresh salad or your favorite sides.

Mom's quiche is a versatile dish that can be enjoyed for breakfast, brunch, lunch, or even dinner. Feel free to customize the fillings with your favorite ingredients and enjoy the creamy, flavorful goodness of homemade quiche!

Dad's Grilled Salmon

Ingredients:

- 4 salmon fillets (about 6 oz each), skin-on
- 2 tablespoons olive oil
- 2 tablespoons soy sauce (or tamari for gluten-free option)
- 2 tablespoons honey
- 2 cloves garlic, minced
- 1 tablespoon lemon juice
- 1 teaspoon Dijon mustard
- Salt and pepper to taste
- Optional: Fresh herbs (such as chopped parsley or dill) for garnish
- Lemon wedges, for serving

Instructions:

1. Prepare the Marinade:
    - In a small bowl, whisk together olive oil, soy sauce, honey, minced garlic, lemon juice, Dijon mustard, salt, and pepper.
2. Marinate the Salmon:
    - Place the salmon fillets in a shallow dish or a large resealable plastic bag. Pour the marinade over the salmon, making sure each fillet is well-coated. Cover or seal the bag and refrigerate for at least 30 minutes, or up to 1 hour. You can also marinate it longer for more flavor.
3. Preheat the Grill:
    - Preheat your grill to medium-high heat, about 400-450°F (200-230°C). Make sure the grill grates are clean and lightly oiled to prevent sticking.
4. Grill the Salmon:
    - Remove the salmon fillets from the marinade and discard the marinade. Place the salmon fillets skin-side down on the grill. Close the grill lid and cook for about 4-6 minutes, depending on the thickness of the fillets.
5. Flip and Finish Cooking:
    - Carefully flip the salmon fillets using a spatula. Grill for an additional 4-6 minutes, or until the salmon is cooked through and flakes easily with a fork. The internal temperature should reach 145°F (63°C).
6. Serve:
    - Remove the grilled salmon from the grill and transfer to a serving platter. Garnish with fresh herbs if desired and serve immediately with lemon wedges on the side.

7. Enjoy:
    - Dad's Grilled Salmon is ready to be enjoyed! Serve it with your favorite side dishes such as roasted vegetables, rice, or a fresh salad for a complete and delicious meal.

This grilled salmon recipe is versatile and can be adjusted to your taste preferences. It's a healthy and flavorful dish that Dad will be proud to serve to family and friends during gatherings or special occasions.

Aunt Martha's Potatoes Au Gratin

Ingredients:

- 4 large russet potatoes, peeled and thinly sliced (about 1/8 inch thick)
- 2 cups shredded Gruyere cheese (or Swiss cheese)
- 1 cup shredded cheddar cheese
- 2 cups heavy cream
- 2 cloves garlic, minced
- 2 tablespoons unsalted butter
- 1 tablespoon all-purpose flour
- 1/2 teaspoon dried thyme
- Salt and pepper to taste
- Optional: Chopped fresh parsley for garnish

Instructions:

1. Preheat Oven:
    - Preheat your oven to 375°F (190°C). Butter a 9x13-inch baking dish or similar-sized casserole dish.
2. Prepare Potatoes:
    - Peel the potatoes and slice them thinly, about 1/8 inch thick. You can use a mandoline slicer or a sharp knife for even slices.
3. Make the Cheese Sauce:
    - In a saucepan over medium heat, melt the butter. Add minced garlic and sauté for about 1 minute until fragrant.
    - Stir in the flour and cook for another minute, stirring constantly, to make a roux.
    - Gradually whisk in the heavy cream, ensuring there are no lumps. Cook for 5-7 minutes, or until the mixture thickens slightly.
    - Stir in the dried thyme, salt, and pepper to taste. Remove from heat.
4. Layer Potatoes and Cheese:
    - Arrange half of the sliced potatoes in the prepared baking dish, overlapping slightly. Sprinkle half of the shredded Gruyere cheese and half of the shredded cheddar cheese evenly over the potatoes.
    - Pour half of the cream mixture over the cheese and potatoes.
5. Repeat Layers:
    - Layer the remaining sliced potatoes on top. Sprinkle the remaining Gruyere and cheddar cheese over the potatoes.
    - Pour the remaining cream mixture evenly over the top.

6. Bake:
    - Cover the baking dish with aluminum foil and bake in the preheated oven for 45 minutes.
7. Uncover and Finish Baking:
    - Remove the foil and bake for an additional 20-25 minutes, or until the potatoes are tender and the top is golden brown and bubbly.
8. Rest and Serve:
    - Remove Aunt Martha's Potatoes Au Gratin from the oven and let it rest for 10 minutes before serving. Garnish with chopped fresh parsley if desired.
9. Enjoy:
    - Serve Aunt Martha's Potatoes Au Gratin hot as a delicious side dish alongside roasted meats, poultry, or as a main course with a side salad.

This recipe for Potatoes Au Gratin results in creamy, cheesy potatoes with a golden crust, capturing the comforting essence of Aunt Martha's classic dish. It's sure to be a hit at your next family gathering or holiday meal!

Cousin Sarah's Spinach Dip

Ingredients:

- 1 (10 oz) package frozen chopped spinach, thawed and drained
- 1 (8 oz) package cream cheese, softened
- 1 cup sour cream
- 1/2 cup mayonnaise
- 1 cup shredded mozzarella cheese
- 1/4 cup grated Parmesan cheese
- 1 clove garlic, minced
- 1/2 teaspoon onion powder
- 1/2 teaspoon salt
- 1/4 teaspoon black pepper
- Optional: 1/4 teaspoon red pepper flakes (for a hint of heat)
- Optional: 1/2 cup chopped artichoke hearts (drained if canned)
- Optional: 1/2 cup chopped water chestnuts (for crunch)

Instructions:

1. Prepare the Spinach:
    - Thaw the frozen chopped spinach according to package instructions. Once thawed, place in a fine-mesh sieve or colander and press down to drain excess water. You can also use paper towels to squeeze out excess moisture.
2. Mix Ingredients:
    - In a large mixing bowl, combine softened cream cheese, sour cream, mayonnaise, shredded mozzarella cheese, grated Parmesan cheese, minced garlic, onion powder, salt, pepper, and red pepper flakes if using. Stir until well combined and smooth.
3. Add Spinach and Optional Ingredients:
    - Stir in the drained spinach until evenly distributed throughout the mixture.
    - If using optional ingredients like chopped artichoke hearts or water chestnuts, gently fold them into the dip mixture.
4. Chill (Optional):
    - For best flavor, cover the spinach dip and refrigerate for at least 1 hour, allowing the flavors to meld together.
5. Serve:
    - Transfer Cousin Sarah's Spinach Dip to a serving bowl. You can serve it cold or at room temperature.

6. Enjoy:
    - Serve the spinach dip with your favorite dippers such as tortilla chips, crackers, breadsticks, or fresh vegetable sticks.

Cousin Sarah's Spinach Dip is creamy, cheesy, and packed with flavor, making it a crowd-pleasing appetizer for any occasion. Customize it with your favorite additions and enjoy this delicious dip with friends and family!

Uncle Joe's Corn on the Cob

Ingredients:

- Fresh corn on the cob (as many as needed)
- Butter, softened
- Salt and pepper, to taste
- Optional: Fresh herbs (such as parsley or chives), grated Parmesan cheese, or chili powder for seasoning

Instructions:

1. Prepare the Corn:
    - Peel back the husks of the corn, leaving them attached at the base. Remove the silk (the stringy part) from the corn and discard.
2. Soak (Optional):
    - If desired, soak the corn in cold water for about 15-30 minutes. This helps to keep the corn moist while grilling or baking.
3. Grill or Bake the Corn:
Grilling Method:
    - Preheat your grill to medium-high heat.
    - Place the corn on the grill and cook, turning occasionally, until the kernels are tender and lightly charred, about 10-15 minutes in total. Close the lid while cooking, if using a grill.
4. Oven Method:
    - Preheat your oven to 400°F (200°C).
    - Wrap each corn cob individually in aluminum foil.
    - Place the wrapped corn directly on the oven rack and bake for 20-25 minutes, or until the corn is tender.
5. Season the Corn:
    - Once cooked, carefully unwrap the corn (if baked) or remove from the grill.
    - Spread softened butter over each ear of corn, ensuring it melts into the kernels.
    - Season with salt and pepper to taste. You can also sprinkle with fresh herbs, grated Parmesan cheese, or chili powder for added flavor.
6. Serve:
    - Serve Uncle Joe's Corn on the Cob hot as a side dish or as part of a barbecue or summer meal.

Enjoy the sweetness and freshness of Uncle Joe's Corn on the Cob, prepared simply to highlight the natural flavors of the corn with just a touch of seasoning. It's a perfect addition to any outdoor gathering or family dinner!

Sister Emily's Lemon Bars

Ingredients:

For the Crust:

- 1 cup unsalted butter, softened
- 1/2 cup granulated sugar
- 2 cups all-purpose flour
- 1/4 teaspoon salt

For the Lemon Filling:

- 1 1/2 cups granulated sugar
- 1/4 cup all-purpose flour
- 4 large eggs
- 2/3 cup freshly squeezed lemon juice (about 4-5 lemons)
- Zest of 1 lemon
- Powdered sugar, for dusting

Instructions:

1. Preheat Oven:
    - Preheat your oven to 350°F (175°C). Grease or line a 9x13-inch baking dish with parchment paper, leaving an overhang for easy removal.
2. Make the Crust:
    - In a mixing bowl, beat together softened butter and granulated sugar until light and fluffy. Add flour and salt, and mix until the dough comes together and forms a crumbly mixture.
    - Press the dough evenly into the bottom of the prepared baking dish. Use the back of a spoon or your hands to smooth it out.
3. Bake the Crust:
    - Bake the crust in the preheated oven for 15-20 minutes, or until lightly golden brown around the edges. Remove from the oven and set aside.
4. Prepare the Lemon Filling:
    - In another mixing bowl, whisk together granulated sugar and flour. Add eggs, lemon juice, and lemon zest. Whisk until smooth and well combined.
5. Assemble and Bake:
    - Pour the lemon filling over the baked crust, spreading it out evenly.
6. Bake Again:

- Return the baking dish to the oven and bake for an additional 20-25 minutes, or until the filling is set and the edges are lightly golden brown.

7. **Cool and Chill:**
   - Remove from the oven and let Sister Emily's Lemon Bars cool completely in the baking dish on a wire rack. Once cooled, refrigerate for at least 1-2 hours to chill and set.

8. **Serve:**
   - Lift the lemon bars out of the baking dish using the parchment paper overhang. Dust with powdered sugar.
   - Cut into squares or bars using a sharp knife. Enjoy chilled or at room temperature.

Sister Emily's Lemon Bars are tangy, sweet, and perfect for any occasion. They're a refreshing treat that's sure to brighten up your day! Adjust the sweetness or tartness to your preference by varying the amount of sugar or lemon juice.

Brother Mike's Salsa

Ingredients:

- 6 medium ripe tomatoes, diced
- 1/2 red onion, finely chopped
- 1 jalapeño pepper, seeded and finely chopped (adjust amount to taste)
- 1/4 cup chopped fresh cilantro
- 2 cloves garlic, minced
- Juice of 1 lime
- 1 teaspoon ground cumin
- Salt and pepper to taste

Instructions:

1. Prepare the Ingredients:
   - Dice the tomatoes and finely chop the red onion and jalapeño pepper. If you prefer a milder salsa, you can remove the seeds and membranes from the jalapeño before chopping.
2. Combine Ingredients:
   - In a mixing bowl, combine the diced tomatoes, chopped red onion, chopped jalapeño pepper, chopped cilantro, minced garlic, lime juice, and ground cumin.
3. Season to Taste:
   - Season the salsa with salt and pepper to taste. Adjust the amount of jalapeño for more or less heat according to your preference.
4. Chill (Optional):
   - For best flavor, cover the salsa and refrigerate for at least 30 minutes to allow the flavors to meld together. This step is optional but recommended.
5. Serve:
   - Stir Brother Mike's Salsa before serving to ensure the flavors are well mixed. Serve it with tortilla chips as an appetizer, or use it as a topping for tacos, grilled meats, quesadillas, or salads.
6. Enjoy:
   - Enjoy Brother Mike's Salsa fresh and homemade, with its vibrant flavors adding a delicious kick to your favorite dishes!

This salsa recipe is versatile, and you can customize it by adding ingredients like diced avocado, corn, or black beans for extra texture and flavor. It's perfect for gatherings or simply enjoying as a snack with chips. Adjust the ingredients to your taste and enjoy the freshness of homemade salsa made with Brother Mike's recipe!

Grandma's Stuffed Peppers

Ingredients:

- 6 large bell peppers (any color), tops removed and seeds discarded
- 1 lb ground beef (you can also use ground turkey or chicken)
- 1 cup cooked rice (white or brown)
- 1 small onion, finely chopped
- 2 cloves garlic, minced
- 1 can (14.5 oz) diced tomatoes, drained
- 1 cup shredded mozzarella cheese (or any cheese of your choice), divided
- 1 tablespoon tomato paste
- 1 teaspoon dried oregano
- 1 teaspoon dried basil
- Salt and pepper, to taste
- Fresh parsley or basil, chopped, for garnish (optional)

Instructions:

1. Preheat Oven:
    - Preheat your oven to 350°F (175°C). Prepare a baking dish large enough to hold all the stuffed peppers.
2. Prepare the Peppers:
    - Bring a large pot of water to a boil. Add the bell peppers and blanch them for about 3-5 minutes, until slightly softened. Remove them from the water and drain upside down on paper towels.
3. Make the Filling:
    - In a large skillet, cook the ground beef over medium heat until browned. Drain any excess fat.
    - Add the chopped onion and minced garlic to the skillet with the ground beef. Cook for 2-3 minutes until the onion is translucent.
4. Combine Ingredients:
    - Stir in the cooked rice, drained diced tomatoes, half of the shredded cheese, tomato paste, dried oregano, dried basil, salt, and pepper. Mix well until everything is combined and heated through.
5. Stuff the Peppers:
    - Arrange the blanched bell peppers upright in the prepared baking dish. Spoon the meat and rice mixture evenly into each pepper, pressing gently to pack the filling.
6. Bake:

- Cover the baking dish with foil and bake in the preheated oven for 30 minutes.
7. Add Cheese and Bake Again:
    - Remove the foil from the baking dish. Sprinkle the remaining shredded cheese evenly over the tops of the stuffed peppers.
    - Bake, uncovered, for an additional 15-20 minutes, or until the peppers are tender and the cheese is melted and lightly browned.
8. Serve:
    - Remove Grandma's Stuffed Peppers from the oven and let them cool slightly. Garnish with chopped fresh parsley or basil if desired, and serve hot.
9. Enjoy:
    - Serve Grandma's Stuffed Peppers as a delicious and comforting meal on their own, or with a side salad or crusty bread.

These stuffed peppers are filled with savory goodness and make a satisfying meal that the whole family will enjoy. They can be prepared ahead of time and baked when ready to serve, making them perfect for busy weeknights or gatherings. Adjust the ingredients and seasonings to your taste and enjoy Grandma's classic recipe!

Mom's Eggplant Parmesan

Ingredients:

- 2 medium-sized eggplants
- Salt
- 2 cups marinara sauce (homemade or store-bought)
- 2 cups shredded mozzarella cheese
- 1 cup grated Parmesan cheese
- 1 cup all-purpose flour
- 3 large eggs, beaten
- 1 cup Italian-style breadcrumbs
- 1/2 cup vegetable oil, for frying
- Fresh basil leaves, chopped, for garnish (optional)

Instructions:

1. Prepare the Eggplant:
   - Slice the eggplants into 1/4-inch thick rounds. Place the slices in a colander and sprinkle them generously with salt. Let them sit for about 30 minutes to draw out the bitter juices. Rinse the eggplant slices under cold water and pat them dry with paper towels.
2. Set Up Breading Station:
   - Prepare three shallow bowls: one with flour, one with beaten eggs, and one with breadcrumbs.
3. Bread the Eggplant:
   - Dredge each eggplant slice in the flour, shaking off any excess. Dip it into the beaten eggs, allowing any excess to drip off. Then coat it evenly with breadcrumbs, pressing gently to adhere.
4. Fry the Eggplant:
   - In a large skillet, heat vegetable oil over medium heat. Fry the breaded eggplant slices in batches until golden brown on both sides, about 2-3 minutes per side. Place them on paper towels to drain excess oil.
5. Assemble the Eggplant Parmesan:
   - Preheat your oven to 375°F (190°C). Spread a thin layer of marinara sauce on the bottom of a 9x13-inch baking dish.
   - Arrange a layer of fried eggplant slices over the sauce. Top each slice with a spoonful of marinara sauce, a sprinkle of shredded mozzarella cheese, and grated Parmesan cheese. Repeat the layers until all the ingredients are used, finishing with a layer of cheese on top.

6. **Bake:**
    - Cover the baking dish with aluminum foil and bake in the preheated oven for 25-30 minutes, or until the cheese is melted and bubbly.
7. **Serve:**
    - Remove Mom's Eggplant Parmesan from the oven and let it cool slightly. Garnish with chopped fresh basil leaves if desired.
    - Serve hot as a main dish, accompanied by a side of pasta or a green salad.

Mom's Eggplant Parmesan is a comforting and flavorful dish that's perfect for family dinners or entertaining guests. It can be prepared ahead of time and baked when ready to serve, making it convenient for busy schedules. Enjoy the crispy breaded eggplant slices layered with marinara sauce and gooey cheese—a true Italian favorite!

Dad's Paella

Ingredients:

- 1 lb chicken thighs or breasts, bone-in and skin-on, cut into smaller pieces
- 1 lb large shrimp, peeled and deveined
- 1 lb mussels, cleaned and debearded (discard any that are open or do not close when tapped)
- 1 lb chorizo sausage, sliced
- 2 cups Spanish Bomba rice (or Arborio rice as a substitute)
- 4 cups chicken broth
- 1 onion, finely chopped
- 4 cloves garlic, minced
- 1 red bell pepper, thinly sliced
- 1 tomato, diced
- 1/2 cup frozen peas
- 1/2 teaspoon saffron threads (optional)
- 1 teaspoon smoked paprika
- 1 teaspoon sweet paprika
- Salt and pepper to taste
- Olive oil
- Lemon wedges, for serving
- Fresh parsley, chopped, for garnish

Instructions:

1. Prepare the Chicken and Shrimp:
   - Season the chicken pieces with salt and pepper. In a large paella pan or skillet, heat olive oil over medium-high heat. Brown the chicken pieces on all sides until golden brown. Remove and set aside.
   - In the same pan, add the shrimp and cook for about 2 minutes per side, until pink and cooked through. Remove and set aside.
2. Cook the Chorizo and Vegetables:
   - Add the sliced chorizo to the pan and cook until lightly browned. Remove and set aside.
   - In the same pan, add a bit more olive oil if needed. Sauté the chopped onion, minced garlic, and sliced red bell pepper until softened, about 5 minutes.
   - Stir in the diced tomato, smoked paprika, sweet paprika, and saffron threads (if using). Cook for another 2-3 minutes until fragrant.

3. Add the Rice and Broth:
    - Add the Bomba rice to the pan, stirring to coat it in the oil and spices. Cook for 1-2 minutes until the rice is slightly toasted.
    - Pour in the chicken broth and bring to a simmer. Season with salt and pepper to taste. Arrange the chicken pieces, shrimp, chorizo, and mussels (hinge side down) on top of the rice mixture.
4. Simmer and Cook:
    - Reduce the heat to medium-low and let the paella simmer, uncovered, for about 20-25 minutes, or until the rice is cooked and most of the liquid has been absorbed. Avoid stirring the rice during this time to allow the bottom to develop a crispy crust (socarrat).
5. Add Peas and Finish Cooking:
    - Sprinkle the frozen peas evenly over the paella during the last 5 minutes of cooking. Cover the paella with foil or a lid to steam the peas.
6. Serve:
    - Once the rice is tender and the liquid has been absorbed, remove the paella from heat. Discard any mussels that have not opened.
    - Garnish Dad's Paella with chopped fresh parsley and serve hot with lemon wedges on the side for squeezing over individual portions.

Dad's Paella is a flavorful and impressive dish that brings the essence of Spanish cuisine to your table. It's perfect for special occasions or gatherings with family and friends, showcasing a delicious blend of seafood, meat, and aromatic spices in every bite. Enjoy this homemade paella with a glass of Spanish wine for a truly authentic experience!

Aunt Martha's Corn Chowder

Ingredients:

- 4 cups fresh corn kernels (about 4-5 ears of corn) or frozen corn kernels
- 4 slices bacon, chopped
- 1 medium onion, diced
- 2 stalks celery, diced
- 1 red bell pepper, diced
- 2 cloves garlic, minced
- 2 medium potatoes, peeled and diced
- 4 cups chicken or vegetable broth
- 1 cup heavy cream
- 1/2 teaspoon dried thyme
- 1/2 teaspoon smoked paprika
- Salt and pepper to taste
- Chopped fresh parsley or chives, for garnish (optional)

Instructions:

1. Cook the Bacon:
    - In a large soup pot or Dutch oven, cook the chopped bacon over medium heat until crispy. Remove the bacon with a slotted spoon and set aside on a paper towel-lined plate.
2. Sauté Vegetables:
    - In the same pot with the bacon drippings, add the diced onion, celery, and red bell pepper. Sauté for 5-6 minutes, or until the vegetables are softened.
3. Add Garlic and Potatoes:
    - Stir in the minced garlic and diced potatoes. Cook for another 2-3 minutes, stirring occasionally.
4. Simmer Chowder:
    - Pour in the chicken or vegetable broth, scraping any browned bits from the bottom of the pot. Bring the mixture to a boil, then reduce the heat to medium-low. Cover and simmer for 10-15 minutes, or until the potatoes are tender.
5. Blend Soup (Optional):
    - If you prefer a thicker consistency, use an immersion blender to partially blend the soup, leaving some chunks of vegetables intact. Alternatively, remove about 2 cups of the soup and blend in a blender until smooth, then return it to the pot.

6. Add Corn and Cream:
   - Add the fresh or frozen corn kernels to the pot. Stir in the heavy cream, dried thyme, smoked paprika, salt, and pepper. Simmer for an additional 5-7 minutes, or until the corn is tender and the soup is heated through.
7. Adjust Seasoning:
   - Taste and adjust the seasoning with salt and pepper as needed.
8. Serve:
   - Ladle Aunt Martha's Corn Chowder into bowls. Garnish with crispy bacon pieces, chopped fresh parsley or chives if desired.

Aunt Martha's Corn Chowder is best served hot, accompanied by crusty bread or crackers. It's a comforting soup that captures the sweetness of corn and the richness of cream, perfect for cooler evenings or anytime you crave a hearty and satisfying meal. Enjoy this homemade chowder with family and friends!

Cousin Sarah's Fruit Salad

Ingredients:

- 2 cups fresh strawberries, hulled and halved
- 1 cup fresh blueberries
- 1 cup fresh raspberries
- 1 cup fresh blackberries
- 2 cups fresh pineapple chunks
- 2 cups fresh mango chunks
- 1 cup green grapes, halved
- 1 cup red grapes, halved
- 1-2 tablespoons honey or maple syrup (optional, for added sweetness)
- Juice of 1-2 limes or lemons
- Fresh mint leaves, chopped or whole, for garnish (optional)

Instructions:

1. Prepare the Fruits:
    - Wash and prepare all the fresh fruits as needed. Cut larger fruits like strawberries, pineapple, and mango into bite-sized pieces.
2. Combine Fruits:
    - In a large mixing bowl, combine the strawberries, blueberries, raspberries, blackberries, pineapple chunks, mango chunks, and halved grapes.
3. Add Sweetener and Citrus Juice:
    - Drizzle honey or maple syrup (if using) over the mixed fruits. Squeeze the juice of 1-2 limes or lemons over the fruit salad to add a citrusy flavor and prevent the fruits from browning. Gently toss to combine.
4. Chill (Optional):
    - For best flavor, cover the fruit salad and refrigerate for at least 30 minutes to allow the flavors to meld together.
5. Serve:
    - Before serving, garnish Cousin Sarah's Fruit Salad with chopped or whole fresh mint leaves for a burst of freshness and color.
6. Enjoy:
    - Serve the fruit salad chilled as a refreshing side dish or dessert. It's perfect for picnics, barbecues, brunches, or any gathering where you want to serve a healthy and delicious treat.

Cousin Sarah's Fruit Salad is versatile, and you can customize it by adding your favorite fruits or adjusting the sweetness to your taste. Enjoy the vibrant colors and flavors of this delightful fruit salad made with fresh and nutritious ingredients!

Uncle Joe's Coleslaw

Ingredients:

- 1 small head of cabbage, finely shredded (about 6-8 cups)
- 2 medium carrots, grated
- 1/2 cup mayonnaise
- 1/4 cup sour cream or plain yogurt
- 2 tablespoons apple cider vinegar or white vinegar
- 1 tablespoon Dijon mustard
- 1 tablespoon honey or granulated sugar
- 1/2 teaspoon celery seed (optional)
- Salt and pepper, to taste

Instructions:

1. Prepare the Vegetables:
    - Finely shred the cabbage using a sharp knife or a mandoline slicer. Grate the carrots using a box grater or a food processor fitted with a grating attachment.
2. Make the Dressing:
    - In a large mixing bowl, whisk together mayonnaise, sour cream or yogurt, vinegar, Dijon mustard, honey or sugar, celery seed (if using), salt, and pepper. Adjust seasoning to taste.
3. Combine Ingredients:
    - Add the shredded cabbage and grated carrots to the bowl with the dressing.
4. Mix Well:
    - Toss the vegetables with the dressing until evenly coated. Use a spoon or clean hands to mix thoroughly, ensuring all the cabbage and carrots are coated with the dressing.
5. Chill (Optional):
    - For best results, cover the coleslaw and refrigerate for at least 1 hour before serving. This allows the flavors to meld together and the cabbage to slightly soften.
6. Serve:
    - Stir Uncle Joe's Coleslaw before serving to redistribute the dressing. Serve chilled as a side dish or topping for sandwiches, burgers, or tacos.
7. Enjoy:

- Enjoy the crunchy and creamy texture of Uncle Joe's Coleslaw as a refreshing addition to any meal or gathering.

This coleslaw recipe can be easily adjusted to your taste preferences. You can add extras like chopped apples, raisins, or nuts for additional texture and flavor. It's a versatile dish that complements a wide range of main dishes and is always a hit at picnics, barbecues, and potlucks.

Sister Emily's Rice Krispie Treats

Ingredients:

- 6 cups crispy rice cereal (such as Rice Krispies)
- 4 tablespoons unsalted butter
- 1 package (10 oz) marshmallows (about 40 large marshmallows)

Instructions:

1. Prepare the Pan:
    - Lightly grease a 9x13-inch baking pan or line it with parchment paper.
2. Melt the Butter and Marshmallows:
    - In a large pot or saucepan, melt the butter over low heat. Add the marshmallows and stir constantly until completely melted and smooth. Remove from heat as soon as the marshmallows are melted to avoid overcooking.
3. Mix in the Cereal:
    - Add the crispy rice cereal to the melted marshmallow mixture. Stir quickly until the cereal is evenly coated with the marshmallow mixture.
4. Press into Pan:
    - Transfer the mixture into the prepared baking pan. Use a greased spatula or wax paper to press the mixture firmly and evenly into the pan.
5. Let Cool and Set:
    - Allow Sister Emily's Rice Krispie Treats to cool at room temperature for at least 30 minutes, or until firm and set.
6. Cut and Serve:
    - Cut into squares or rectangles using a sharp knife. Serve and enjoy these delicious treats!

Variations:

- Flavor Additions: Add vanilla extract or almond extract to the melted marshmallow mixture for extra flavor.
- Mix-Ins: Stir in chocolate chips, M&M's, chopped nuts, or sprinkles into the cereal mixture before pressing into the pan.
- Decorate: Drizzle melted chocolate or frosting on top of the cooled treats for a decorative touch.

Sister Emily's Rice Krispie Treats are perfect for any occasion, from school lunches to birthday parties. They're quick to make and loved by both kids and adults alike for their crispy, marshmallowy goodness. Enjoy making and sharing these nostalgic treats!

Brother Mike's Deviled Eggs

Ingredients:

- 6 large eggs
- 1/4 cup mayonnaise
- 1 teaspoon Dijon mustard
- 1/2 teaspoon white vinegar or lemon juice
- Salt and pepper, to taste
- Paprika, for garnish
- Optional: Chopped fresh chives or parsley for garnish

Instructions:

1. Boil the Eggs:
    - Place the eggs in a single layer in a saucepan and cover with water, about 1 inch above the eggs. Bring to a boil over medium-high heat.
    - Once boiling, cover the saucepan with a lid, remove from heat, and let the eggs sit in the hot water for 12 minutes.
2. Cool and Peel the Eggs:
    - Transfer the eggs to a bowl of ice water and let them cool for a few minutes. This helps in easy peeling.
    - Gently tap each egg on a hard surface and roll to crack the shell. Peel off the shell under cool running water. Pat dry with paper towels.
3. Prepare the Filling:
    - Slice each egg in half lengthwise. Carefully remove the yolks and place them in a small bowl.
    - Mash the egg yolks with a fork until smooth. Add mayonnaise, Dijon mustard, vinegar or lemon juice, salt, and pepper. Mix until well combined and creamy. Adjust seasoning to taste.
4. Fill the Egg Whites:
    - Spoon or pipe the yolk mixture back into the egg white halves, dividing evenly.
5. Garnish and Serve:
    - Sprinkle Brother Mike's Deviled Eggs with paprika for color and optional chopped fresh chives or parsley for added freshness.
6. Chill (Optional):
    - For best flavor, refrigerate the deviled eggs for at least 30 minutes to allow the flavors to meld together before serving.
7. Enjoy:

- Serve Brother Mike's Deviled Eggs as a delicious appetizer or snack. They are perfect for parties, potlucks, or any gathering where you want to impress with a classic and tasty dish!

These deviled eggs are versatile, and you can adjust the filling to your taste by adding ingredients like pickle relish, hot sauce, or diced herbs. They're a timeless favorite that's sure to please everyone!

Grandma's Baked Ziti

Ingredients:

- 1 lb ziti pasta (or penne rigate)
- 1 lb ground beef or Italian sausage (optional)
- 1 onion, finely chopped
- 3 cloves garlic, minced
- 1 jar (24-26 oz) marinara sauce or homemade tomato sauce
- 1 cup ricotta cheese
- 1 cup shredded mozzarella cheese
- 1/2 cup grated Parmesan cheese
- 1/4 cup chopped fresh basil or parsley
- Salt and pepper, to taste
- Olive oil

Instructions:

1. Preheat Oven:
   - Preheat your oven to 375°F (190°C). Grease a 9x13-inch baking dish with olive oil or non-stick spray.
2. Cook the Pasta:
   - Cook the ziti pasta in a large pot of salted boiling water according to package instructions until al dente. Drain and set aside.
3. Prepare the Sauce:
   - In a large skillet or saucepan, heat olive oil over medium heat. Add the chopped onion and cook until softened, about 5 minutes. Add the minced garlic and cook for another 1-2 minutes until fragrant.
   - If using ground beef or Italian sausage, add it to the skillet and cook until browned, breaking it up into smaller pieces with a spoon.
   - Pour in the marinara sauce and stir to combine. Simmer the sauce for 10-15 minutes to allow the flavors to meld together. Season with salt and pepper to taste.
4. Combine Pasta and Sauce:
   - In a large mixing bowl, combine the cooked ziti pasta and the prepared sauce. Mix well until the pasta is evenly coated with sauce.
5. Assemble the Baked Ziti:
   - Spread half of the pasta mixture evenly into the prepared baking dish. Dollop half of the ricotta cheese over the pasta in small spoonfuls.

> Sprinkle half of the shredded mozzarella and grated Parmesan cheeses over the top.
> - Repeat with the remaining pasta mixture, ricotta cheese, and shredded cheeses.

6. Bake:
   - Cover the baking dish with aluminum foil and bake in the preheated oven for 20 minutes. Remove the foil and bake for an additional 10-15 minutes, or until the cheese is melted and bubbly and the edges are lightly browned.
7. Rest and Serve:
   - Remove Grandma's Baked Ziti from the oven and let it cool for a few minutes before serving. Sprinkle chopped fresh basil or parsley over the top for garnish, if desired.
8. Enjoy:
   - Serve Grandma's Baked Ziti hot as a delicious and comforting main dish. It pairs well with a crisp green salad and garlic bread.

Grandma's Baked Ziti is a crowd-pleasing dish that's perfect for family gatherings, potlucks, or anytime you crave a satisfying Italian meal. The combination of pasta, savory sauce, and melted cheeses creates a dish that's sure to evoke warm memories and hearty enjoyment.

Mom's Beef Wellington

Ingredients:

- 1 ½ - 2 pounds beef tenderloin
- Salt and pepper, to taste
- 2 tablespoons olive oil
- 2 tablespoons Dijon mustard
- 1 package puff pastry (2 sheets), thawed if frozen
- 8-10 slices prosciutto or Parma ham
- 1 pound mushrooms, finely chopped
- 2 cloves garlic, minced
- 1 tablespoon fresh thyme leaves
- 2 tablespoons butter
- 1 egg, beaten (for egg wash)

Instructions:

1. Prepare the Beef:
   - Season the beef tenderloin generously with salt and pepper.
   - Heat olive oil in a large skillet over high heat. Sear the beef on all sides until well-browned, about 2 minutes per side. Remove from heat and let it cool slightly.
2. Coat with Mustard:
   - Brush the seared beef tenderloin all over with Dijon mustard. Set aside.
3. Prepare the Mushroom Duxelles:
   - In the same skillet, melt butter over medium heat. Add minced garlic and chopped mushrooms. Cook until mushrooms release their moisture and become golden brown, about 8-10 minutes.
   - Season with salt, pepper, and fresh thyme leaves. Remove from heat and let it cool.
4. Assemble the Wellington:
   - Lay out a large sheet of plastic wrap. Arrange the slices of prosciutto or Parma ham on the plastic wrap, overlapping them slightly to create a sheet.
   - Spread the mushroom duxelles evenly over the prosciutto.
5. Wrap the Beef:
   - Place the seared beef tenderloin in the center of the mushroom-covered prosciutto.

- Using the plastic wrap to help you, tightly roll the prosciutto and mushroom mixture around the beef, forming a log shape. Twist the ends of the plastic wrap to secure. Refrigerate for 15-20 minutes to firm up.

6. **Prepare the Pastry:**
   - Preheat the oven to 400°F (200°C).
   - On a lightly floured surface, roll out the puff pastry sheets. Place one sheet on a baking tray lined with parchment paper.

7. **Assemble and Bake:**
   - Unwrap the beef tenderloin from the plastic wrap and place it in the center of the puff pastry sheet on the baking tray.
   - Brush the edges of the pastry with beaten egg.
   - Carefully fold the pastry over the beef, sealing the edges and trimming any excess pastry if necessary. Brush the entire pastry with beaten egg for a golden finish.

8. **Bake:**
   - Bake in the preheated oven for 35-40 minutes, or until the pastry is golden brown and the beef reaches your desired level of doneness (for medium-rare, aim for an internal temperature of about 130-135°F / 55-57°C).

9. **Rest and Serve:**
   - Remove from the oven and let it rest for 10 minutes before slicing. Serve your mom's delicious Beef Wellington with sides like roasted vegetables, mashed potatoes, or a fresh salad.

Enjoy your meal! This dish is perfect for special occasions and always impresses guests.

Dad's Shish Kabobs

Ingredients:

- 1 ½ pounds beef sirloin or lamb, cut into 1-inch cubes
- 1 red bell pepper, cut into chunks
- 1 green bell pepper, cut into chunks
- 1 yellow bell pepper, cut into chunks
- 1 large red onion, cut into chunks
- 1 zucchini, sliced into thick rounds
- Cherry tomatoes
- Mushrooms (optional)
- Wooden or metal skewers

Marinade:

- ⅓ cup olive oil
- ⅓ cup soy sauce
- ¼ cup Worcestershire sauce
- 2 tablespoons red wine vinegar
- 2 cloves garlic, minced
- 1 tablespoon Dijon mustard
- 1 tablespoon honey
- 1 teaspoon dried oregano
- 1 teaspoon dried basil
- 1 teaspoon paprika
- Salt and pepper, to taste

Instructions:

1. Prepare the Marinade:
    - In a bowl, whisk together olive oil, soy sauce, Worcestershire sauce, red wine vinegar, minced garlic, Dijon mustard, honey, oregano, basil, paprika, salt, and pepper.
2. Marinate the Meat:
    - Place the cubed meat in a large resealable plastic bag or a bowl. Pour the marinade over the meat, making sure it is well coated. Seal the bag or cover the bowl and refrigerate for at least 1 hour, or preferably overnight.
3. Prepare the Skewers:

- If using wooden skewers, soak them in water for at least 30 minutes to prevent them from burning on the grill.
            - Preheat the grill to medium-high heat.
    4. Assemble the Kabobs:
        - Thread the marinated meat and assorted vegetables onto skewers, alternating for color and variety.
    5. Grill the Kabobs:
        - Lightly oil the grill grates to prevent sticking. Place the skewers on the preheated grill.
        - Grill the kabobs, turning occasionally, until the meat is cooked to your desired doneness and the vegetables are tender and lightly charred, about 10-12 minutes for medium-rare beef (adjust cooking time based on your preference and the thickness of the meat).
    6. Serve:
        - Remove the kabobs from the grill and let them rest for a few minutes.
        - Serve Dad's delicious shish kabobs hot, optionally garnished with fresh herbs like parsley or cilantro. They pair well with rice, couscous, or grilled bread.

Enjoy your Dad's flavorful shish kabobs! It's a great dish for summer gatherings or any time you're in the mood for tasty grilled skewers.

Aunt Martha's Shepherd's Pie

Ingredients:

- 1 ½ pounds ground lamb or beef
- 1 onion, finely chopped
- 2 cloves garlic, minced
- 2 carrots, diced
- 1 cup frozen peas
- 1 cup frozen corn
- 2 tablespoons tomato paste
- 1 tablespoon Worcestershire sauce
- 1 cup beef or vegetable broth
- Salt and pepper, to taste
- 2 tablespoons olive oil
- Fresh thyme or rosemary, chopped (optional)

For the Mashed Potatoes:

- 2 pounds potatoes (Russet or Yukon Gold), peeled and cut into chunks
- ½ cup milk or cream
- 4 tablespoons butter
- Salt and pepper, to taste
- 1 cup shredded cheddar cheese (optional)

Instructions:

1. Prepare the Mashed Potatoes:
    - Place the peeled and chopped potatoes in a large pot of salted water. Bring to a boil and cook until tender, about 15-20 minutes. Drain well.
    - Mash the potatoes with a potato masher or fork. Add butter, milk (or cream), salt, and pepper. Mash until smooth and creamy. Stir in shredded cheddar cheese if using. Set aside.
2. Make the Filling:
    - Preheat oven to 400°F (200°C).
    - In a large skillet or pan, heat olive oil over medium heat. Add chopped onion and cook until softened, about 5 minutes.
    - Add minced garlic and diced carrots. Cook for another 3-4 minutes until carrots begin to soften.

- Push the vegetables to the side of the pan and add the ground lamb or beef. Cook, breaking up with a spoon, until browned and cooked through.
- Stir in tomato paste, Worcestershire sauce, and fresh thyme or rosemary (if using). Cook for 1-2 minutes until fragrant.
- Add frozen peas and corn. Pour in beef or vegetable broth. Bring to a simmer and cook for 5-7 minutes until the mixture has thickened slightly. Season with salt and pepper to taste.

3. Assemble and Bake:
    - Transfer the meat and vegetable mixture to a baking dish (9x13 inches or similar size).
    - Spread the mashed potatoes evenly over the top of the meat mixture, smoothing with a spatula.
4. Bake:
    - Place the baking dish in the preheated oven and bake for 25-30 minutes, or until the mashed potatoes are lightly golden and the filling is bubbly around the edges.
5. Serve:
    - Remove from the oven and let it cool for a few minutes before serving. Garnish with additional fresh herbs if desired.

Enjoy Aunt Martha's comforting Shepherd's Pie straight from the oven. It's a complete meal in itself, but you can serve it with a side salad or steamed vegetables if you like.

Cousin Sarah's Garlic Bread

Ingredients:

- 1 loaf of French bread or Italian bread
- ½ cup unsalted butter, softened
- 4 cloves garlic, minced (adjust to taste)
- 2 tablespoons fresh parsley, finely chopped (optional)
- Salt, to taste
- Freshly ground black pepper, to taste
- 1 cup shredded mozzarella cheese (optional)

Instructions:

1. Prepare the Garlic Butter:
   - In a small bowl, combine softened butter, minced garlic, chopped parsley (if using), salt, and black pepper. Mix well until all ingredients are evenly incorporated.
2. Prepare the Bread:
   - Preheat your oven to 375°F (190°C).
   - Slice the loaf of French or Italian bread in half lengthwise. Place both halves cut-side up on a baking sheet lined with parchment paper or aluminum foil.
3. Spread the Garlic Butter:
   - Spread the prepared garlic butter evenly over the cut sides of the bread. Make sure to cover the entire surface for maximum flavor.
4. Optional: Add Cheese (if desired):
   - Sprinkle shredded mozzarella cheese evenly over the garlic buttered bread, if using. This step adds a delicious cheesy layer to your garlic bread.
5. Bake the Garlic Bread:
   - Place the baking sheet with the garlic bread into the preheated oven.
   - Bake for 10-12 minutes, or until the bread is toasted and the cheese (if added) is melted and bubbly.
6. Serve:
   - Remove from the oven and let it cool slightly before slicing. Cut into individual slices and serve warm alongside pasta dishes, soups, or as a tasty appetizer.

Enjoy Cousin Sarah's flavorful garlic bread straight from the oven! It's perfect for sharing with family and friends at any mealtime.

Uncle Joe's Crab Cakes

Ingredients:

- 1 pound lump crab meat, picked over for shells
- 1 cup breadcrumbs (preferably fresh)
- 1/4 cup mayonnaise
- 1 large egg, beaten
- 1 tablespoon Dijon mustard
- 1 tablespoon Worcestershire sauce
- 2 tablespoons chopped fresh parsley
- 1/4 cup finely chopped red bell pepper
- 1/4 cup finely chopped green onion
- 2 cloves garlic, minced
- 1/2 teaspoon Old Bay seasoning (adjust to taste)
- Salt and pepper, to taste
- 2 tablespoons unsalted butter
- 2 tablespoons olive oil
- Lemon wedges, for serving

Instructions:

1. Prepare the Crab Cakes:
    - In a large bowl, combine breadcrumbs, mayonnaise, beaten egg, Dijon mustard, Worcestershire sauce, chopped parsley, chopped red bell pepper, chopped green onion, minced garlic, Old Bay seasoning, salt, and pepper.
    - Gently fold in the lump crab meat, being careful not to break up the crab too much. You want to keep the crab meat in large chunks.
2. Form the Crab Cakes:
    - Shape the mixture into 8 crab cakes, about 1/2 inch thick. You can use a 1/3 cup measuring cup to portion out each cake for even sizing.
3. Chill the Crab Cakes:
    - Place the crab cakes on a baking sheet lined with parchment paper. Cover with plastic wrap and refrigerate for at least 30 minutes. Chilling helps the crab cakes hold their shape when cooking.
4. Cook the Crab Cakes:
    - In a large skillet, heat 1 tablespoon of butter and 1 tablespoon of olive oil over medium heat.
    - Add the crab cakes to the skillet (in batches if necessary to avoid overcrowding) and cook until golden brown and crispy on both sides,

about 4-5 minutes per side. Use the remaining butter and olive oil for the next batch if needed.
5. Serve:
    - Transfer the cooked crab cakes to a serving platter. Serve hot, garnished with lemon wedges on the side for squeezing over the crab cakes.

Enjoy Uncle Joe's delicious crab cakes as a starter or as part of a main course. They pair wonderfully with a fresh salad or some roasted vegetables.

Sister Emily's Oatmeal Cookies

Ingredients:

- 1 cup unsalted butter, softened
- 1 cup brown sugar, packed
- 1/2 cup granulated sugar
- 2 large eggs
- 1 teaspoon vanilla extract
- 1 1/2 cups all-purpose flour
- 1 teaspoon baking soda
- 1/2 teaspoon salt
- 1 teaspoon ground cinnamon
- 3 cups old-fashioned rolled oats
- 1 cup raisins or chocolate chips (optional)

Instructions:

1. Preheat Oven and Prepare Baking Sheets:
    - Preheat your oven to 350°F (175°C). Line baking sheets with parchment paper or silicone baking mats.
2. Cream Butter and Sugars:
    - In a large mixing bowl, cream together the softened butter, brown sugar, and granulated sugar until light and fluffy.
3. Add Eggs and Vanilla:
    - Beat in the eggs one at a time, then add the vanilla extract. Mix well until combined.
4. Combine Dry Ingredients:
    - In a separate bowl, whisk together the flour, baking soda, salt, and ground cinnamon.
5. Combine Wet and Dry Ingredients:
    - Gradually add the dry ingredients to the butter mixture, mixing until just combined.
6. Add Oats (and Optional Add-Ins):
    - Stir in the rolled oats until evenly distributed. If using, gently fold in the raisins or chocolate chips.
7. Form Cookies:
    - Drop tablespoon-sized portions of dough onto the prepared baking sheets, spacing them about 2 inches apart. You can use a cookie scoop for even portions.

8. Bake:
    - Bake in the preheated oven for 10-12 minutes, or until the edges are lightly golden brown.
9. Cool and Serve:
    - Remove from the oven and let the cookies cool on the baking sheets for a few minutes before transferring them to a wire rack to cool completely.
10. Enjoy:
    - Once cooled, enjoy Sister Emily's oatmeal cookies with a glass of milk or your favorite hot beverage.

These oatmeal cookies are sure to be a hit, with their chewy texture and comforting flavors. Feel free to customize them with your favorite mix-ins or nuts for added variety!

Brother Mike's Cheese Platter

Cheese Selection:

1. Hard Cheese: Choose a firm cheese like aged cheddar, Gouda, or Manchego. These cheeses offer a sharp and robust flavor.
2. Soft Cheese: Include a creamy and mild soft cheese such as Brie, Camembert, or a triple cream cheese. These cheeses contrast nicely with the firmer options.
3. Blue Cheese: Add a blue cheese for a pungent and tangy flavor. Options like Roquefort, Gorgonzola, or Stilton are great choices.
4. Specialty Cheese: Consider adding a unique or local cheese that stands out, such as a goat cheese with herbs, smoked cheese, or a flavored cheese.

Accompaniments:

- Crackers and Bread: Choose a variety of crackers and crusty bread slices. Options like water crackers, whole grain crackers, and baguette slices complement different cheese textures.
- Fresh and Dried Fruit: Arrange fresh grapes, berries, figs, or sliced apples and pears. Dried fruits like apricots, figs, or cranberries add sweetness and texture.
- Nuts: Include a selection of nuts such as almonds, walnuts, or pecans. Toasted nuts add a crunchy contrast to the creamy cheeses.
- Honey or Jam: Serve honeycomb or a drizzle of honey for pairing with blue cheese. Fruit preserves or fig jam also complement soft cheeses like Brie.
- Olives and Pickles: Add a small bowl of marinated olives, cornichons, or pickled vegetables for a savory element.

Presentation:

- Arrange cheeses: Place each cheese on a wooden board or serving platter. Label each cheese with its name if desired.
- Create variety: Arrange accompaniments around the cheeses, alternating textures and flavors. Use small bowls or ramekins for jams or honey.
- Garnish: Add fresh herbs like rosemary sprigs or edible flowers for a decorative touch.

Tips:

- Room temperature: Take the cheeses out of the refrigerator about 30 minutes before serving to allow flavors to develop.

- Balance flavors: Aim for a variety of flavors and textures to cater to different tastes.
- Pairing: Consider offering a selection of wines, such as reds like Cabernet Sauvignon or whites like Sauvignon Blanc, to complement the cheese platter.

Creating Brother Mike's Cheese Platter is about offering a delightful array of flavors and textures that guests can enjoy together. Adjust the selection based on your preferences and availability, and have fun assembling a beautiful and delicious spread!

Grandma's Cinnamon Rolls

Ingredients:

For the Dough:

- 1 cup warm milk (110-115°F)
- 2 1/4 teaspoons (1 packet) active dry yeast
- 1/2 cup granulated sugar
- 1/3 cup unsalted butter, melted
- 2 large eggs, at room temperature
- 1 teaspoon salt
- 4 1/2 - 5 cups all-purpose flour

For the Filling:

- 1 cup packed light brown sugar
- 2 1/2 tablespoons ground cinnamon
- 1/3 cup unsalted butter, softened

For the Cream Cheese Frosting:

- 4 ounces cream cheese, softened
- 1/4 cup unsalted butter, softened
- 1 cup powdered sugar
- 1/2 teaspoon vanilla extract
- Pinch of salt

Instructions:

1. Activate the Yeast:
    - In a large mixing bowl, dissolve the yeast and a pinch of sugar in the warm milk. Let it sit for 5-10 minutes until foamy.
2. Make the Dough:
    - To the yeast mixture, add the melted butter, granulated sugar, eggs, salt, and 4 cups of flour. Mix until combined.
    - Gradually add more flour, 1/4 cup at a time, until the dough begins to pull away from the sides of the bowl.
    - Turn the dough out onto a lightly floured surface and knead for about 5-7 minutes until smooth and elastic.
3. First Rise:

- Place the dough in a greased bowl, turning once to coat. Cover with a clean kitchen towel or plastic wrap and let it rise in a warm place until doubled in size, about 1-2 hours.
4. Prepare the Filling:
    - In a small bowl, combine the brown sugar and ground cinnamon for the filling.
5. Roll and Fill the Dough:
    - Punch down the risen dough and roll it out on a lightly floured surface into a 16x21-inch rectangle.
    - Spread the softened butter evenly over the dough, leaving a 1/4-inch border around the edges. Sprinkle the cinnamon-sugar mixture evenly over the butter.
6. Roll Up the Dough:
    - Starting with the long edge, tightly roll up the dough into a log. Pinch the seam to seal.
7. Cut into Rolls:
    - Cut the rolled dough into 12 equal slices using a sharp knife or dental floss. Place the rolls in a greased 9x13-inch baking dish or two 9-inch round pans.
8. Second Rise:
    - Cover the rolls loosely with a clean kitchen towel or plastic wrap and let them rise in a warm place until doubled in size, about 45-60 minutes.
9. Bake:
    - Preheat your oven to 350°F (175°C). Bake the rolls for 25-30 minutes, or until golden brown.
10. Make the Frosting:
    - While the rolls are baking, prepare the cream cheese frosting. In a mixing bowl, beat together the softened cream cheese and butter until smooth.
    - Add powdered sugar, vanilla extract, and a pinch of salt. Beat until creamy and smooth.
11. Frost the Rolls:
    - Remove the cinnamon rolls from the oven and let them cool for a few minutes. Spread the cream cheese frosting evenly over the warm rolls.
12. Serve:
    - Serve Grandma's cinnamon rolls warm. Enjoy their soft, fluffy texture and sweet cinnamon goodness!

These cinnamon rolls are perfect for breakfast or as a comforting treat any time of day. They're sure to evoke fond memories of Grandma's kitchen with every bite!

Mom's Lemon Chicken

Ingredients:

- 4 boneless, skinless chicken breasts
- Salt and pepper, to taste
- 1/2 cup all-purpose flour
- 2 tablespoons olive oil
- 4 cloves garlic, minced
- 1/2 cup chicken broth
- 1/4 cup fresh lemon juice (about 2 lemons)
- Zest of 1 lemon
- 2 tablespoons capers, drained (optional)
- 2 tablespoons unsalted butter
- 2 tablespoons chopped fresh parsley, for garnish

Instructions:

1. Prepare the Chicken:
    - Season the chicken breasts with salt and pepper on both sides. Dredge each chicken breast in flour, shaking off any excess.
2. Cook the Chicken:
    - In a large skillet, heat the olive oil over medium-high heat. Add the chicken breasts and cook for about 4-5 minutes per side, or until golden brown and cooked through (internal temperature of 165°F / 74°C). Remove the chicken from the skillet and set aside.
3. Make the Sauce:
    - In the same skillet, add minced garlic and sauté for about 1 minute until fragrant.
    - Pour in the chicken broth, lemon juice, and lemon zest. Stir to combine, scraping up any browned bits from the bottom of the skillet.
4. Simmer the Sauce:
    - Bring the sauce to a simmer and let it cook for 2-3 minutes until slightly reduced.
5. Add Capers and Butter:
    - If using capers, add them to the skillet. Stir in the butter until melted and the sauce has slightly thickened.
6. Return Chicken to the Skillet:
    - Return the cooked chicken breasts to the skillet, turning to coat them in the lemon butter sauce. Let them heat through for a minute or two.

7. Serve:
    - Transfer the lemon chicken to a serving platter. Spoon some of the sauce over the chicken.
    - Garnish with chopped fresh parsley for a pop of color and freshness.
8. Enjoy:
    - Serve Mom's lemon chicken hot, accompanied by your favorite side dishes like rice, pasta, or roasted vegetables.

This Mom's Lemon Chicken is tangy, savory, and perfect for a family dinner or entertaining guests. The lemony sauce adds a bright and zesty flavor that complements the tender chicken beautifully.

www.ingramcontent.com/pod-product-compliance
Lightning Source LLC
LaVergne TN
LVHW081607060526
838201LV00054B/2124